SELECTED MATERIAL FROM
JUST ENOUGH UNIX
FIFTH EDITION

ENGR 106
Purdue University
2005 — 2006

Paul K. Andersen

New Mexico State University
Las Cruces, NM

Custom Publishing

Boston   Burr Ridge, IL   Dubuque, IA   Madison, WI   New York   San Francisco   St. Louis
Bangkok   Bogotá   Caracas   Lisbon   London   Madrid
Mexico City   Milan   New Delhi   Seoul   Singapore   Sydney   Taipei   Toronto

SELECTED MATERIAL FROM JUST ENOUGH UNIX, FIFTH EDITION
ENGR 106 • Purdue University • 2005 — 2006

This book is a McGraw-Hill Custom Publishing textbook and contains selected chapters from *Just Enough UNIX*, Fifth Edition by Paul K. Andersen. Copyright © 2006, 2003, 2000, 1997, 1993 by The McGraw-Hill Companies, Inc. Reprinted with permission of the publisher. Many custom published texts are modified versions or adaptations of our best-selling textbooks. Some adaptations are printed in black and white to keep prices at a minimum, while others are in color.

2 3 4 5 6 7 8 9 0 PAH PAH 0 9 8 7 6

ISBN 0-256-35752-8

Editor: Julie Kehrwald
Production Editor: Nina Meyer
Cover Designer: Fairfax Hutter
Printer/Binder: P.A. Hutchison Company

Contents

INTRODUCTION TO UNIX

Mention *computer*, and many people are apt to think of *hardware*—the physical device, consisting of circuit boards, a central processing unit (CPU), memory chips, and so on. Equally important, however, is the software—the programs that tell the hardware what to do. Without software, a computer is just a box with wires attached to it.

The operating system is an especially important kind of software that manages the resources of the computer. This chapter provides a brief overview of computer hardware and software, with emphasis on the UNIX operating system.

1.1 Computer Hardware

Computers come in a bewildering range of shapes, sizes, and types. Despite their differences, almost all have four essential components (see Figure 1–1):

■ **Central processing unit (CPU).** The CPU performs calculations and manipulates data. It is the "brain" of the computer.

■ **Main memory (primary memory, internal memory, RAM).** This is the place where the CPU looks for instructions and data to process. Main memory— also called *random-access memory* or *RAM*—is fast but limited in how much it can hold.

■ **Mass storage (external memory, secondary memory).** Information that is not immediately needed by the computer is placed in mass storage or secondary memory, which is usually slower than main memory but can hold much more. The most common mass storage devices are magnetic disks.

■ **Input/output devices.** Input/output (I/O) devices are used to move information to and from the computer. The most common I/O devices include the keyboard, mouse, video display, and printer.

Other devices—such as terminals, printers, scanners, and so on—are sometimes attached to the computer. These are generally called *peripherals*.

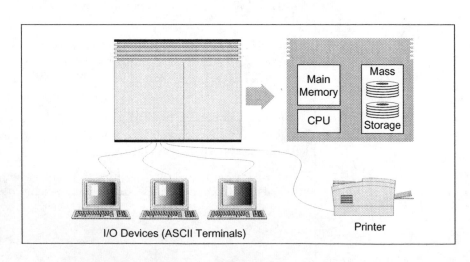

Figure 1-1
A typical computer sys-
tem. The four parts of a
single-user computer
are shown.

1.2 One User or Many?

*Workstations are more
powerful than the typical
personal computer.*

The computer represented in Figure 1–1 is a *single-user* computer, either a *personal computer* or *workstation*. It has one keyboard and one video display, and is intended to serve just one person at a time. This is common with smaller computers.

Large computers, on the other hand, often have more power than one person can profitably use. These computers are commonly set up as *multiuser systems,* as shown in Figure 1–2. Note that the multiuser computer has the same basic parts as the single-user computer: CPU, main memory, mass storage, and I/O devices.

*ASCII is a method for
representing text; it is
discussed in Chapter 18.*

The I/O devices shown in Figure 1–2 are *character* or *ASCII terminals*, each consisting of a keyboard and a video monitor. Such terminals can display text but not graphics, and are affectionately called "dumb" terminals.

`telnet` *is discussed in
Chapters 3 and 22.*

In some cases, a personal computer may be used instead of a dumb terminal to interact with a multiuser system. A *terminal-emulation program* running on the personal computer causes it to behave like an ASCII terminal. A utility called `telnet` allows the computers to communicate with each other.

Figure 1-2
Multiuser computer
system. This system is
set up to handle as many
as three users at a time.
Some large systems can
serve hundreds of users
simultaneously.

Bits, Bytes, Hertz, MIPS, and Flops

Computer memory is usually measured in bits and bytes. *Bit* is short for *binary digit*; a bit can store either a 0 or a 1. A *byte* is a grouping of eight bits; a byte can store a single character. The following prefixes are used for larger quantities:

kilo- (K) "thousand" (10^3)

mega- (M) "million" (10^6)

giga- (G) "billion" (10^9)

Thus, 1 megabyte (Mbyte or MB) is approximately 1 million bytes of memory. A million bytes can hold a million characters, or about 500 typewritten pages.

A CPU may be rated by the number of bits it can process at a time. For example, a 32-bit CPU manipulates 32 bits at a time. Another way to say this is that the CPU has a 32-bit *word size*.

The rate at which words are processed by a CPU is determined by the *clock speed*. The *clock speed* is expressed in megahertz (MHz); 1 megahertz = 1 million pulses per second. Other things being equal, CPUs with larger word sizes and higher clock speeds are faster.

A computer's speed is sometimes expressed in terms of the number of arithmetic operations it can perform in a second. This is measured in *flops*, which is short for *floating-point operations per second*. Alternatively, a computer's speed may be expressed by the number of instructions it can execute in a second. This is measured in *MIPS*, which is short for *millions of instructions per second*.

Sometimes these prefixes are meant as approximations—see Exercise 7.

1.3 Computer Networks

A server is computer hardware (or software) that provides a service to other hardware (or software).

Another way to accommodate multiple users is to link two or more computers together to form a *network*. Figure 1–3 shows a network consisting of three workstations (called *hosts*), a printer, and another computer called a *file server* that has no video display device but does have magnetic disks.

The hosts connected to the network may be full-fledged UNIX workstations, non-UNIX personal computers, or *diskless workstations*. A diskless workstation has only limited secondary memory, relying instead on the magnetic disks attached to the server. (The server serves the workstations by providing mass storage for them.)

Computer networking has become very popular. One reason for this is simple economics. By allowing users to share expensive resources such as printers, a network can be relatively economic to set up and operate.

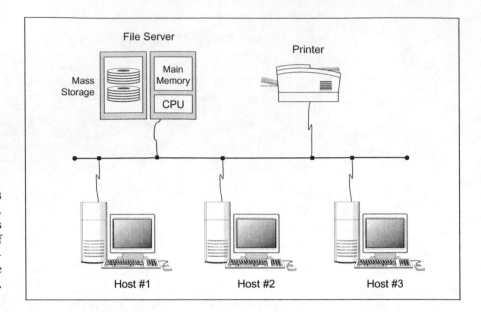

Figure 1-3
Computer network. This network includes four computers, one of which is a server providing disk storage for the other three.

1.4   The Operating System

As important as the computer hardware is, it can do nothing without software. There are two general categories of software. Programs that allow users to solve specific problems are called *applications*. Examples include word processors, spreadsheets, and database management programs.

Software that provides support for creating and running applications is called *systems software*. The most important systems software is the *operating system* (OS), which performs three vital functions:

■ **Interaction with the user**. The OS handles the communication between the user and the computer, passing commands from the user to the computer and returning messages from the computer to the user.

■ **Management of other software**. The OS manages the way other software is stored and run.

■ **Control of peripherals.** The OS controls all of the various peripheral devices (printers, disk drives, terminals, and so on) that are attached to the computer.

1.5   Open and Closed Systems

Some operating systems are *proprietary* or *closed*, meaning they are developed and owned by one company. Most proprietary operating systems are designed to work only on certain types of computer hardware, making them *nonportable*. For example, MS-DOS—the most popular operating system of the 1980s—was written

The Origins of UNIX

The UNIX story begins with a failed operating system, two computer scientists with time on their hands, and a computer game named *Space Travel*. The failed operating system was Multics, a joint venture involving General Electric, MIT, and the AT&T Bell Laboratories. Multics was envisioned as a great technological leap forward: an interactive, multiuser operating system that would be years ahead of anything then available. But the project was too ambitious, and by 1969 it was clear that Multics was in trouble. Reluctantly, Bell Labs withdrew from the project, leaving the Bell researchers with nothing to do.

A Bell researcher named Ken Thompson had written *Space Travel*, a computer game that allowed a Multics user to pilot an imaginary spacecraft to the major bodies of the solar system. While awaiting approval from Bell management for several new research projects, Thompson decided to rewrite *Space Travel* to run on a little-used PDP-7 minicomputer in the lab. He enlisted the aid of Dennis Ritchie, another Bell computer scientist who had worked on the Multics project.

It was no easy task. All programming had to be done on another machine, then transferred to the PDP-7 using punched paper tape. It did not take long for Thompson to wish that the PDP-7 had its own operating system, similar in some respects to Multics, but much simpler. So he wrote one. This was the first UNIX operating system, although it did not acquire that name until the following year. (The name was originally "Unics," a pun on Multics. Later this became UNIX.)

The PDP-7 had only about 9 Kbytes of main memory, less than some of today's household appliances. Thompson and Ritchie requested a larger computer. In exchange, they offered to produce a UNIX-based word-processing system for the Bell Labs patent department. They got their new computer—a PDP-11 with 24 Kbytes of main memory—and delivered the word-processing system in 1971. It was an immediate success, and UNIX was launched.

by Microsoft for machines having an Intel CPU. Likewise, the original Macintosh System was owned solely by Apple Computer and ran only on machines having a Motorola CPU.

In contrast, UNIX is a *nonproprietary* or *open* system. No single company is responsible for the development of UNIX and no single company owns it. Anyone may write an operating system that conforms to the published UNIX specifications. Moreover, UNIX has been adapted to run on a wide variety of computer hardware—in other words, UNIX is a *portable* operating system. Software is said to be portable if it can be moved from one type of computer to another with minimal changes. (This is not to be confused with a portable computer, which is computer hardware designed to be easily carried from place to place.)

UNIX and C

UNIX was originally written in assembly language, a primitive programming language. Since each type of computer has its own assembly language, early versions of UNIX could run only on the PDP-11 and closely related machines. But in 1973, UNIX was rewritten in C, a high-level programming language invented by Dennis Ritchie. It was much easier to write programs in C; just as important, C was designed to be a portable language, not tied to any particular type of computer hardware. As a result, UNIX became a portable operating system.

1.6 Multitasking and Time-Sharing

Background processes can run without interacting with the user.

UNIX is a *multitasking* operating system, meaning it enables the computer to work on more than one task at a time. With UNIX, you can run several programs "in the background" while you work on another task "in the foreground."

How does multitasking work? Although some computers actually can perform more than one task at a time, others cannot. However, by switching rapidly back and forth between tasks, performing a little here and a little there, a computer can create the illusion of doing many things simultaneously. This technique is called *time-sharing*, and it is feasible only because (a) the computer is very fast and (b) UNIX takes care of scheduling what is to be done and when.

UNIX is also capable of interacting with more than one user at a time—in other words, it is a *multiuser* operating system. This capability is especially important on large mainframe computers that must serve a large number of users; without it, everyone would have to wait his or her turn to use the computer.

1.7 Major Components of UNIX

The UNIX operating system consists of four main parts:

Many people consider "operating system" and "kernel" to be synonymous.

■ **Kernel.** The *kernel* is the master control program of the computer. It resides in the computer's main memory, and it manages the computer's resources. It is the kernel that handles the switching necessary to provide multitasking.

The file system is covered in Part II.

■ **File System.** UNIX organizes data into collections called *files*. Files may be grouped together into collections called *directory files* or *directories*.

Shells are covered in Part III.

■ **Shell.** The part of UNIX that interprets user commands and passes them on to the kernel is called the *shell*. A typical shell provides a *command-line interface*, where the user can type commands. This book covers the most common shells: the Bourne Shell, C Shell, TC Shell, Korn Shell, and Bourne-Again Shell (Bash).

■ **Utilities.** A *utility* is a useful software tool that is included as a standard part of the UNIX operating system. Utilities are often called *commands*.

Why So Many Versions of UNIX?

When UNIX was under development at AT&T's Bell Laboratories in the 1970s, AT&T was still prevented by law from competing in the computer industry. Since the company could not make a profit on UNIX, they gave it away, essentially free of charge.

UNIX became very popular at colleges and universities, where it was used for both teaching and research. (The low price tag undoubtedly had something to do with this popularity.) The early versions of UNIX were still quite crude, so academic computer scientists introduced their own improvements. Especially prominent in this effort was the Computer Systems Research Group at the University of California at Berkeley, which began producing its own versions of UNIX. By 1982, Berkeley Software Distribution (BSD) UNIX rivaled the AT&T versions in popularity.

Meanwhile, many computer companies produced their own versions of UNIX, often borrowing features from both AT&T and Berkeley UNIX. Of course, each version had its own name, usually ending in *x* (AIX, A/UX, HP-UX, Irix, Ultrix, and XENIX, to mention a few.) At one time there were as many as 200 variants of UNIX on the market.

1.8 Versions of UNIX

See "Why So Many Versions of UNIX?", this page.

When we say UNIX, we are really talking about a family of operating systems. In general, UNIX systems can trace their ancestry to AT&T System V UNIX, Berkeley Software Distribution (BSD) UNIX, or various UNIX-like systems:

■ **System V UNIX**. Most of the major commercial UNIX systems on the market today are based on AT&T UNIX, including AIX, Irix, Solaris, Tru64, Unicos, and UnixWare.

■ **BSD UNIX**. A number of operating systems have been derived from 4.4 BSD-Lite, the ultimate version of BSD UNIX, which was released in 1994. The most prominent of these are BSD/OS, FreeBSD, MacOS X, NetBSD, and OpenBSD.

■ **UNIX-like systems**. The UNIX-like operating systems (also called *work-alikes* or *clones*) behave very much like other UNIX systems, but do not use any software from AT&T. This category includes Hurd, Linux, Minix, and XINU.

Incidentally, the question is often asked, is it UNIX or Unix? Both forms are encountered. Since 1971, the name has been UNIX (all caps). However, this is now a trademark of the Open Group, and should properly be applied only to systems that are certified by that organization. For that reason, some people write Unix (mixed case) to refer to the entire family of operating systems, certified or not. In this book, we adhere to the earlier tradition and write UNIX throughout.

Linux and Other UNIX-Like Systems

In the early 1980s, AT&T still restricted the commercial use of the UNIX system. This led some companies to write their own operating systems that mimicked the behavior of UNIX without using any of AT&T's source code. These included systems such as Coherent, Idris, and Uniflex.

As UNIX spread in academia, it became popular for computer science courses on operating systems. Eventually, however, AT&T decided to restrict access to the internal code of UNIX. As a result, a number of computer science professors independently developed their own UNIX-like systems for teaching. The most prominent of these were Douglas Comer's XINU ("Xinu Is Not UNIX") and Andy Tanenbaum's Minix.

In 1991, a 21-year-old Finnish student named Linus Torvalds created his own operating system based on Minix. This became Linux, a UNIX-like system for personal computers. This system has proven to be an enormous success. Linux is available at no charge from the Free Software Foundation. Hundreds of volunteer programmers worldwide work to maintain and extend Linux.

1.9 UNIX Standards

See "A Brief History of UNIX Standardization" on page 11.

Traditionally, most UNIX systems have been similar enough that a person who learned to use one would have little trouble using any of the others. Even so, the differences could be irksome. A program might run well on one UNIX system but not on another, or it might give different results. This was an especially challenging problem for software vendors and organizations (such as the U. S. government) that had to maintain a variety of computer systems.

To address the problem of software portability, the Institute of Electrical and Electronics Engineers (IEEE) devised the Portable Operating System Interface (POSIX) standards to define how a standard operating system should behave. Systems and utilities which conform to the POSIX standards are said to be "POSIX-compliant." Most current UNIX systems are POSIX-compliant.

Another important organization promoting UNIX standardization is The Open Group, which actually owns the UNIX trademark. Before a company may apply the UNIX brand name to an operating system, that system must conform to the Single UNIX Specification defined by The Open Group.

1.10 Windows and Graphical User Interfaces

It is difficult to take full advantage of a multitasking operating system like UNIX if you can only see output from one process at a time on your monitor. Fortunately, most recent UNIX systems have the ability to divide the monitor screen into multiple areas called *windows* (Figure 1–4), each of which acts as if it

A Brief History of UNIX Standardization

Although similar in most respects, the many versions of UNIX were different enough to cause headaches for programmers, vendors, and users. For this reason, efforts began in the mid-1980s to define a UNIX standard.

In 1983, The Institute of Electrical and Electronics Engineers (IEEE) began work on a series of Portable Operating System Interface (POSIX) standards. The first POSIX standard was formally adopted by the American National Standards Institute (ANSI) in 1988. Most vendors of UNIX operating systems have modified their systems in accordance with the POSIX standards.

In 1984, the X/Open organization was created by several leading European computer companies. X/Open had as its mission the promotion of open (nonproprietary) operating systems, especially UNIX.

The Open Software Foundation (OSF), a consortium of major UNIX vendors (including IBM, Hewlett-Packard, and DEC) was formed in 1988. Its goal was to produce an alternative to AT&T UNIX that was not controlled by any one company.

AT&T was also aware of the need for standardization. In 1989, AT&T System V Release 4 (abbreviated "SVR4") was released. SVR4 combined the best features of the four most popular UNIX derivatives, which were SVR3, 4.3BSD, SunOS, and Microsoft XENIX.

In 1993, Novell acquired UNIX Systems Laboratories from AT&T. Later that year, Novell transferred ownership of the UNIX brand name to the X/Open organization. In 1995, Novell sold its UNIX business, including the UNIX source code (but not the UNIX trademark), to SCO.

In 1996, X/Open merged with the OSF to form The Open Group. As owner of the UNIX trademark, The Open Group defines the Single UNIX Specification, a set of standards that an operating system must meet to use the UNIX name.

In 1999, IEEE and The Open Group announced a joint effort to revise both the POSIX and the Single UNIX Specification. The revised standards were formally adopted by the International Organization for Standardization (ISO) in 2003.

were a separate monitor. Using a windowing system, you could read your electronic mail in one window, compose a reply in another window, and run a spreadsheet program from a third window, all at the same time.

The typical windowing system also offers what is called a *graphical user interface* (GUI or "gooey"), which allows you to work with pictures as well as character data. To run a particular program under a GUI, you might use a pointing device such

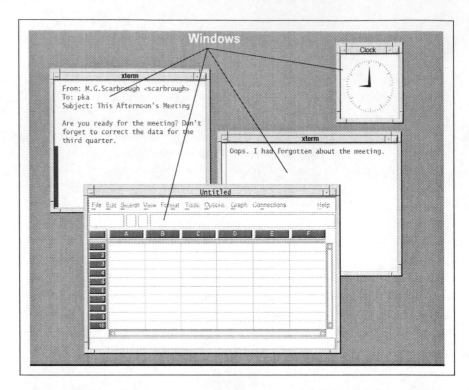

Figure 1-4
A windowing display.
Four windows are
shown; each window
acts as an independent
output device.

as a mouse to select an *icon* (a symbol) that represents that program, rather than having to remember and type a command. Because most people find it easier to work with pictures and pointing devices, GUIs have become very popular.

If you have used an Apple Macintosh or a PC running Microsoft Windows, you are already familiar with windows and GUIs. On UNIX systems, the GUI is usually based on the X Window System ("X" for short), which was originally developed at the Massachusetts Institute of Technology.

A server is software (or
hardware) that provides a
service to other software (or
hardware).

The X Window System works according to what is called a *client-server model*. In other words, X acts as a server for other programs (the clients) by providing a graphical user interface for them. This makes X especially well suited to networked computing because the clients and server can run on separate computers.

1.11 The Window Manager

Although the X Window System makes it possible to create a graphical user interface, X does not specify what the windows must look like or how they are manipulated by the user. That is the job of a program called the *window manager*. The window manager determines the "look and feel" of the GUI, controlling the appearance of the windows and determining how those windows are opened, closed, sized, resized, and moved.

Dozens of window managers have been created. The following are commonly used:

■ **Tab Window Manager** (twm). Originally developed at MIT and supplied as part of the X Window System, twm is a "plain vanilla" window manager that offers few frills. Even so, experienced UNIX programmers like twm because it can be configured to suit their personal tastes.

■ **Virtual Window Manager** (fvwm). Popular with Linux users, fvwm is free software derived from twm.

■ **Open Look Window Manager** (olwm). Sun Microsystems was the strongest promoter of Open Look, which has not been generally adopted by other manufacturers.

You will see how to begin using Motif in Chapter 4.

■ **Motif Window Manager** (mwm). Motif was developed by the Open Software Foundation (OSF), a consortium of several leading UNIX vendors. Motif was designed to have a "look and feel" similar to that of the IBM Presentation Manager and Microsoft Windows, two widely used GUIs for personal computers.

■ **Desktop Window Manager** (dtwm). Based on Motif, the Desktop Window Manager was developed for the Common Desktop Environment (discussed below).

1.12   Desktop Environment

The plethora of UNIX windowing systems has been a cause of confusion for system administrators and users. In 1993, six of the largest UNIX vendors started the Common Open Software Environment (COSE) initiative to address this problem. The result was the Common Desktop Environment (CDE).

You will see how to start using CDE in Chapter 5.

CDE is designed to provide a consistent look and feel, regardless of the variety of UNIX being used. The CDE user interface is organized around the idea of a "desktop," using *icons* or pictures to represent items—such as documents, files, and file folders—that might be found on a real desk. This approach is familiar to users of the Apple Macintosh and the Microsoft Windows operating systems. CDE also provides a new set of standard software tools, including a text editor, a calendar/datebook, and an electronic mail tool, in addition to the traditional UNIX utilities.

Other desktop environments are available, including the K Desktop Environment (KDE), the GNU Network Object Model Environment (Gnome), and XFce.

1.13   X Terminals

The X Window System was designed to be portable. As a result, X runs on virtually every kind of computer, from Macintoshes and PCs to supercomputers. This has contributed greatly to its success.

However, X will not run on a conventional character terminal—a terminal that can display text but not graphics—because considerable computing power is required to support a graphical user interface. This has led to the development of a hybrid input/output device called an *X terminal*, which has a CPU and enough internal memory to run X, but is not a complete computer in itself. (Most X terminals lack disk drives, for instance.) An X terminal is more expensive than a character-based terminal, but less expensive than a complete UNIX workstation.

Instead of purchasing an X terminal, many users run *X-terminal emulation programs* on their personal computers. Such programs allow a personal computer to act as if it were an X terminal.

1.14 Remote Access

Many users wish to connect to their UNIX system when working remotely (for example, while at home or traveling). Figure 1-5 shows four ways to do this.

Modem is short for "modulator-demodulator." Figure 1-5(a) shows a personal computer and a UNIX system communicating using two modems. A *modem* converts outgoing digital data into signals for transmission over ordinary telephone lines (a process known as *modulation*). The receiving modem then converts the incoming telephone signals into digital form (*demodulation*).

The Internet is discussed in Part V. Figure 1-5(b) shows another arrangement involving a personal computer and a standard modem. In this case, the modem communicates with an Internet Service Provider (ISP), which provides an Internet connection to the UNIX system.

Conventional modems are relatively slow. Figure 1-5(c) shows a system that provides faster data transmission. *Digital Subscriber Line* (DSL) technology uses sophisticated data-compression methods to transmit data at high rates over telephone lines.

Figure 1-5(d) shows another system for achieving faster data transmission rates. Some cable television companies provide data transmission over their coaxial cables using a special *cable modem*.

Other methods are used for gaining access to a remote computer system, including wireless and satellite technology. For more information about remote access, see the *Just Enough UNIX* website (`www.mhhe.com/andersen`).

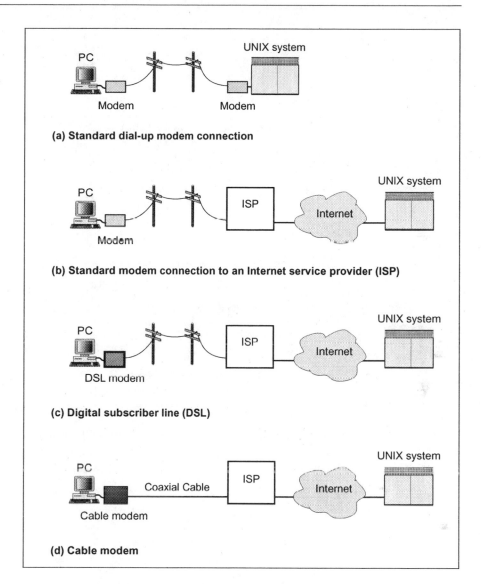

Figure 1-5
Remote access to a
UNIX system.

1.15   Exercises

1. Be sure you can define the following terms:

hardware	word size	shell
software	clock speed	file
CPU	flops	file system
main memory	MIPS	directory
secondary memory	server	utility
mass storage	client	command

external memory	host	window
I/O device	operating system	GUI
peripheral	proprietary	icon
network	portable OS	window manager
bit	open system	X terminal
byte	multitasking	terminal emulation
kilo-	time-sharing	modem
mega-	clone	ISP
giga-	kernel	DSL

2. What are the four main hardware components of most computer systems?

3. What are the main components of the UNIX operating system?

4. Name the most common UNIX shells.

5. Name the most commonly used X window managers.

6. Name three UNIX desktop environments.

7. When referring to the capacity of a computer's memory, computer scientists often use prefixes like kilo-, mega-, and giga- only approximately. For example, a kilobyte of memory is not exactly 1,000 bytes, but rather 2^{10} bytes. Likewise, a megabyte is really 2^{20} bytes, and a gigabyte is really 2^{30} bytes. What is the difference between a thousand and 2^{10}? A million (10^6) and 2^{20}? A billion (10^9) and 2^{30}?

YOUR UNIX ACCOUNT

Tutorials related to this chapter are found in Chapters 3, 4, and 5.

In one respect, UNIX is like your local bank. Just as you need a bank account to withdraw money (legally) from a bank, you also need an account to use a UNIX computer. In this chapter, you will learn what you need to know to obtain and begin using a UNIX account.

2.1 Your System Administrator

Every bank has a manager who sets bank policy, opens and closes customer accounts, balances the books, and generally sees that the bank operates smoothly. Of course, the manager does not necessarily do all of these things personally, but the manager is responsible to see that someone does.

Similarly, most UNIX installations have a *system administrator*, who sees that the system runs smoothly (most of the time, anyway). The system administrator's duties include

- Setting up the hardware;

- Installing software, including the UNIX operating system;

- Starting up the system (and shutting it down when necessary);

- Monitoring system usage;

- Backing up users' files;

- Creating new user accounts; and

- Troubleshooting.

The system administrator does not necessarily do all of these things personally—large computer installations typically divide these duties among several persons. Thus, when you read "system administrator," think "the system administrator or one of his or her assistants."

2.2 Your Account Name

A large UNIX installation may serve hundreds or thousands of users, each having his or her own account. To identify these accounts, each is given a unique name, which is typically based in some way on the user's real name or nickname. For example, the following would all be likely account names for a user named John P. Jones:

```
jpjones
jonesjp
jones
johnp
jpj
sparky
```

The policies for assigning account names vary. In some organizations, the system administrator chooses the name for you; in others, you may choose your own, subject to certain rules. The following rules are fairly typical:

■ Select a name that is at least three characters long, but no more than eight characters long.

■ Be sure that no other account has the same name.

■ Choose an account name that is related in some way to your real name or a nickname.

■ Use only numbers and lowercase letters; do not include uppercase letters or punctuation.

When you start a work session on the computer, you will be asked to *log in* by giving your account name:

```
login:
```

Because you use your account name when logging in, your account name is often referred to as your *login name* or *login*.

2.3 Your Password

Your login name is public knowledge. To prevent unauthorized use of your account, the computer also asks you for a secret *password*:

```
password:
```

By entering your password, you verify to the computer that you really are the person to whom the account belongs.

The system administrator will probably choose your first password for you. After that, you can (and should) choose your own passwords. A good password is one that is easy for you to remember, but difficult for someone else to guess. Here are some good general guidelines for selecting a password:

Your particular computer installation may have other rules as well—consult your system administrator.

■ Choose a password that is at least six characters long. (Passwords can be as long as you like, but some systems only examine the first eight characters.)

■ Combine numbers, upper- and lowercase letters, and punctuation.

■ Make the password memorable, but avoid common names and any words that might be found in a dictionary.

■ Do not use your social security number, your telephone number, your login, or any variation (forward or backward) of your login.

■ Make sure a new password differs significantly from the old one.

A number of strategies exist for choosing a password. One is to misspell an easily remembered word or name. For example, neither `Chicago` nor `chicago` would be acceptable as passwords. But the following deliberate misspellings would be:

Do not use these examples—think up your own password.

`ch1Kagoh`

`Ch!.CAGO`

`Sh33?kago`

Another strategy is to form a password from the first letter of each word in an easily remembered phrase. Including punctuation is a good idea. For example:

`NiMyyd!` (**N**ot **i**n **My** **y**ard you **d**on't!)

`Ihnybtf` (**I** **h**ave **n**ot **y**et **b**egun **t**o **f**ight)

`H,hotr` (**H**ome, **h**ome **o**n **t**he **r**ange)

`wtdatap` (**w**here **t**he **d**eer **a**nd **t**he **a**ntelope **p**lay)

Your password is the main line of protection for your account. Anyone who discovers your password can do nearly anything to your account—including deleting all of your files. Therefore, it is extremely important that you keep your password secure.

WARNING	MEMORIZE YOUR PASSWORD—DO NOT WRITE IT DOWN. AND NEVER DIVULGE YOUR PASSWORD TO ANYONE.

You will see how to change your password in the next chapter.

If you suspect that someone else has learned your password, you should change it immediately. In fact, it may be a good idea to change your password occasionally in any case, just to be safe.

2.4   Other Account Information

When your account is created, the system administrator sets up the following information in addition to the login name and password:

■ **Home Directory.** Your home directory is the place where all of your other files and directories reside. The home directory has a name, which is the same as your login name.

■ **Group ID.** You may be assigned to a group of users. In some organizations, groups are set up so that users in the same department or working on the same projects can easily share fles.

■ **Login Shell.** The system administrator will select a shell to start up automatically whenever you log in.

When you receive your UNIX account, be sure to ask what groups (if any) you have been assigned to and what your login shell is.

2.5   More Questions to Ask

There are a number of additional questions to ask your system administrator:

■ Which version of UNIX will I be using?

■ What kind of terminal will I be using? What is its `terminfo` code?

■ What are the erase, interrupt, stop, and continue keys?

■ Which printer(s) may I use?

■ How can I gain remote access to the system?

The rest of this chapter will explain what each of these questions means.

2.6   Versions of UNIX

You may recall that the name UNIX refers to a family of operating systems, most derived from either AT&T System V or Berkeley Software Distribution (BSD) UNIX. In addition, there are various UNIX-like systems in common use:

■ **System V UNIX:** AIX, Irix, Solaris, Tru64 Unix, Unicos, UnixWare

■ **BSD UNIX:** BSD/OS, Mac OS X, NetBSD, OpenBSD, ULTRIX

■ **UNIX-like systems:** Hurd, Linux, Minix, XINU

Ask your system administrator which kind of UNIX you will be using, and whether it is based on System V or BSD UNIX (or a UNIX-like system).

2.7   Termcap and Terminfo

As an open system, UNIX must be able to work with a wide variety of I/O devices. The UNIX system includes a database describing the operating characteristics of the many different terminals it can use. This is called either the `terminfo` ("terminal information") or `termcap` ("terminal capabilities") database.

When you log in, your system may request that you indicate the type of terminal device you are using by specifying its `terminfo` (or `termcap`) code. For example, suppose you were using a DEC VT 100 terminal. The code for this terminal is

`vt100`

Ask your system administrator which `terminfo` code(s) you should know, if any.

2.8   Special Keys

Figure 2-1 shows a typical computer keyboard. It has the same letter, number, and punctuation keys as a typewriter. It also has a number of special keys not found on the traditional typewriter. The following five keys are of particular interest:

■ ⟨RETURN⟩ Also called the ⟨ENTER⟩ or ⟨NEWLINE⟩ key, this is used to send commands to the shell.

■ ⟨ESCAPE⟩ This key, which may be labeled ⟨ESC⟩, is usually found near the upper left corner of the keyboard.

■ ⟨ERASE⟩ Various keys are used to erase characters. On many systems, this function is performed by a ⟨BACKSPACE⟩ or ⟨DELETE⟩ key, or by a combination of keys.

■ ⟨BREAK⟩ This key is (rarely) used during the login procedure.

■ ⟨CONTROL⟩ This may be labeled ⟨Ctrl⟩ on some terminals. It is used in combination with other keys to perform special functions.

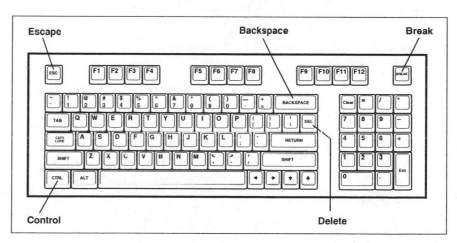

Figure 2-1
A computer keyboard,
showing some of the
special keys.

Of these, the (CONTROL) key deserves special mention. A large number of UNIX commands are executed by holding down the (CONTROL) key while simultaneously pressing another key. For example, on many terminals the erase function can be invoked by the key combination

(CONTROL)—(H)

When referring to this key combination in print, you will often see the notation ^H, where the caret (^) stands for the (CONTROL) key.

Later in the book, you will learn about many of the functions that involve the (CONTROL) key. For now, there are four special functions that you should ask about:

Your system administrator can tell you which keys perform these functions.

Function	Purpose	Key Combination		Alternative
erase	deletes a character	(CONTROL)—(H)	(^H)	(BACKSPACE)
interrupt	stops a program	(CONTROL)—(C)	(^C)	(DELETE)
stop	freezes the terminal	(CONTROL)—(S)	(^S)	?
continue	unfreezes the terminal	(CONTROL)—(Q)	(^Q)	?

Note that there may be more than one way to delete a character or interrupt a program. As shown in Appendix A, UNIX provides a way for you to change the keys that invoke these functions.

2.9 Printer Codes

Almost every UNIX system has a printer for producing paper output. (Paper output is called *hardcopy*.) A large computer installation may have many printers. Individual printers are identified by a code name, which typically reflects the type and location of the device. For example, suppose that one of the printers connected to your UNIX system were an HP LaserJet 4000, located in Room 12. The system administrator might give this printer one of the following code names:

```
hp4000-12
```

```
laserjet12
```

```
room12hp
```

You get the idea. There are no standard rules on naming printers, so it is a good idea to ask your system administrator for the names of the printers that are accessible from your system.

Teletypes and Terminals

When Thompson and Ritchie rewrote UNIX to run on the PDP-11 for the Bell Patent Department, the primary input/output devices were Teletype terminals. These were slow, noisy electromechanical devices that produced their output on rolls of paper.

The Teletype keyboard had the usual typewriter keys for upper- and lowercase letters, numbers, and punctuation. It also had a special "Control" key that was used in combination with other keys to perform special functions. (For example, holding down the Control key and typing the letter *B* caused a bell to ring.)

Although Teletypes are now obsolete, they are not entirely forgotten. The keyboards of newer I/O devices still have a Control key that is used in combination with other keys to perform special functions. In the vocabulary of UNIX, the abbreviation `tty` (short for Teletype) is still used to mean "terminal." And "print" is still used to mean "display output on a terminal," even for terminals that print to a video screen rather than paper.

2.10   Remote Access

The tutorials in Chapters 3, 4, and 5 presume that you will be working directly with your UNIX account using a terminal, a personal computer emulating a terminal, or a UNIX workstation.

However, you may need to work on your UNIX account remotely—while you are on the road, for instance. Remote access usually requires additional hardware and software that is beyond the scope of this book. Ask your UNIX system administrator or Internet Service Provider (ISP) about remote access:

- What hardware and software do you recommend I use for remote access?
- Is dial-up access available? If so, what telephone number(s) should I use?
- What is the procedure for remote access?
- Is there anything else I need to know?

Additional information on remote access can be found on the *Just Enough UNIX* web site (`www.mhhe.com/andersen`).

2.11 Exercises

1. Be sure you can define the following terms:

system administrator	home directory	`termcap` code
account name	group	control key
login name	login shell	interrupt
login	BSD	`tty`
logging in	System V	print
password	`terminfo` code	hardcopy

2. What version of UNIX will you be using? Is it based on AT&T or on BSD UNIX, or is it a UNIX-like system?

3. How are login names assigned for users on your system? Are you allowed to choose your own login, or is one chosen for you?

4. What are the rules for choosing a password on your system? Keeping those rules in mind, choose two or three passwords to use later. (Do not write down your passwords or divulge them to anyone.)

5. Which of the following would be good passwords for someone named Glynda Jones Davis, whose login name, phone number, and social security number are `gjdavis`, 555-2525, and 632-10-6854, respectively? Explain your reasoning.

`cat`	`Glynda7`	`tylerTwo`
`Smith`	`sivagjg`	`t555s632`
`5552525`	`Jones`	`532106854`
`KRoo2`	`jones`	`kangaroo`
`7cattz`	`NotSmith`	`trouble`
`Glynda`	`tiPPecanoe`	`trubble`

6. What kind of terminal will you be using? What is its `terminfo` (or `termcap`) code?

7. Which keys are used to erase input, interrupt a program, freeze the terminal, and unfreeze the terminal?

8. Which printer may you use? What is its code name?

9. What is the procedure for gaining remote access to your account?

Chapter

6

THE UNIX FILE SYSTEM

Tutorials related to this
chapter are found in
Chapters 7, 8, and 9.

The *file system* is the part of UNIX that organizes and keeps track of data. In this chapter, you will learn how to use the UNIX file system to manage your data.

6.1 Files and Directories

If you have previously used a computer, you are undoubtedly familiar with files. Most computer users know that a *file* is a collection of related information—anything from a chocolate cake recipe to a computer program—which is stored in secondary memory.

To UNIX, everything is a file.

UNIX expands the usual definition of *file* to include anything from which data can be taken or to which data can be sent. Hence, a file may be something stored in secondary memory; but it can also refer to the various input/output devices (keyboard, video display, printer, and so on) that can provide or accept data. Since that describes virtually everything the operating system deals with, it is often said that everything is a file to UNIX.

There are three general kinds of UNIX files:

■ **Ordinary files.** These are the common computer files, what people usually have in mind when they say "files." Most of your work on UNIX will involve ordinary files, which are also called *regular files*.

■ **Special files.** Also called *device files*, special files represent physical devices such as terminals, printers, and other peripherals. Although you will frequently use special files, you will rarely (if ever) create or modify one.

■ **Directory files.** Ordinary and special files are organized into collections called *directory files* or *directories*. Whereas ordinary files hold information, directories can hold other files and directories.

You will most often work with ordinary files and directory files, so those will be the focus of this chapter.

6.2   Binary and Text Files

Ordinary UNIX files can be divided into two categories:

■ **Text files.** As the name suggests, a *text file* contains information in the form of text that you can read. Such files can be created and modified using a program called a *text editor*. Because text is generally represented by ASCII code, text files are often called *ASCII files*.

■ **Binary files.** A *binary file* is an ordinary file containing non-textual data. In most cases, binary files are intended to be read and processed by computer programs rather than human users. (If you were to attempt to read or modify binary code using a conventional text editor, its contents would appear undecipherable.)

6.3   Home and Working Directories

When you first log into your UNIX account, you enter what is known as your *home directory*. This is where you will keep any files or directories that you create. The name of your home directory is usually the same as your login name.

After you have logged into your home directory, you are free to move to other directories in the system. Whichever directory you happen to be working in at the time is called your *current directory* or *working directory*. When you first log in, your working directory is your home directory.

Each user on the system is given a home directory. On a typical large UNIX system, there may be hundreds of these home directories, each containing scores of other files and directories.

6.4   The UNIX File Tree

Figure 6-1 is a simplified diagram of a typical UNIX system. It looks something like an upside-down tree, with its root at the top. In fact, the directory at the very top, the one that contains all of the other directories, is called the *root*. Various other directories reside inside the root directory:

bin   This directory contains the software for the shell and the most commonly used UNIX commands. Although bin is short for "binary," you may want to think of it as a "bin" for holding useful software tools.

dev   The name is short for "devices"; this directory holds the special files needed to operate peripheral devices such as terminals and printers.

etc   Various administrative files are kept in this directory, including the list of users that are authorized to use the system, as well as their passwords.

home   Users' home directories are kept here. On some large systems there may be several directories holding user files.

tmp   Temporary files are often kept in this directory.

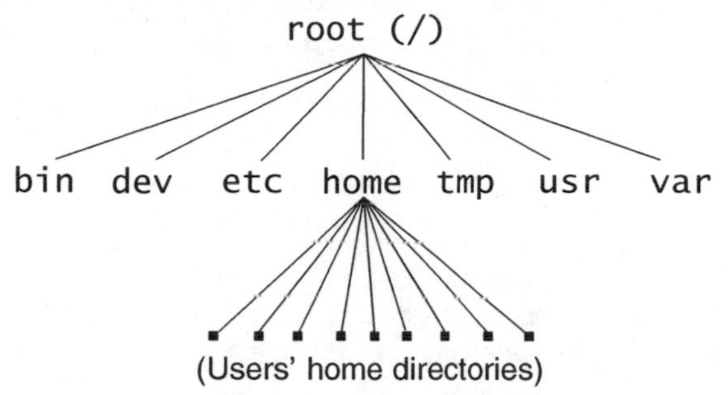

Figure 6-1
Directory structure of a
typical UNIX system.
Users' home directories
are kept in the directory
home in this system.

usr   Some versions of UNIX keep users' home directories in usr; others keep such useful things as the on-line manual pages here.

var   Files containing information that varies frequently are kept in the var directory. An example would be user mailboxes, which are typically found in the /var/mail directory.

Although your particular UNIX system may be set up a bit differently, all UNIX systems have a root directory at the top.

A directory will sometimes be referred to as the "parent" or the "child" of another directory. For example, root is the parent of bin, dev, etc, home, tmp, usr, and var; these directories, in turn, are the children of root. (Child directories are often called *subdirectories*.) Note that every directory except root has exactly one parent, but may have many children.

6.5 File and Directory Names

Every file and directory has a name. The name of your home directory is usually the same as your login, and you normally cannot rename it. However, you must choose names for any other files and directories you make. On most UNIX systems, file names may comprise from one to 255 of the following characters, in any combination:

Some older systems limit
file names to 14 characters.

- Uppercase letters (A to Z);

- Lowercase letters (a to z);

- Numerals (0 to 9);

- Period (.), underscore (_), and comma (,).

A space or a special
character in a file name is
likely to confuse the shell.

In most cases, you should avoid file names that contain spaces or any of the following special characters:

& * \ | [ ] { } $ < > ( ) # ? ' " / ; ^ ! ~ %

Also, avoid using UNIX command names as file names.

It is a good idea to choose descriptive names that give an idea about the contents of the file. Some users also prefer short file names (to save typing).

Consider using *filename extensions*. A filename extension is a suffix attached to the file name to identify the data kept in the file. An extension typically consists of a few characters separated from the rest of the file name by a period. For example, if you were writing a book, you might put each chapter in its own file:

Some non-UNIX operating systems do not allow long filename extensions or multiple extensions.

```
mybook.ch1
mybook.ch1.v2
mybook.ch2
mybook.ch3.revised
mybook.appendix1.old
```

This book follows the convention that ordinary file names are given in lowercase letters, while directory names inside users' home directories are capitalized. This will help you distinguish at a glance directories from ordinary files. You do not have to observe this convention with your own files and directories.

6.6 Absolute Pathnames

To use a file in your current directory, all you need is the file's name. However, if the file is located in another directory, you will need to know the file's *pathname*. A pathname is an address that shows the file's position in the file system.

An absolute pathname shows how to find a file, beginning at the root.

Absolute or *full* pathnames give the location of a file in relation to the top of the file system. The simplest full pathname is for the root directory, which is represented by a slash:

```
/
```

The absolute pathnames for the root's child directories, shown in Figure 6–1, are

```
/bin              /dev              /etc
/home             /tmp              /usr
/var
```

All absolute pathnames begin with a slash.

Note that each of these begins with a slash (/), which tells you that the path starts at the root. Note too that this is a *forward* slash, not a backslash (\).

Figure 6–2 shows home and two of the users' home directories it contains (jack and jill). You have already seen that the pathname for home is

```
/home
```

The absolute pathname for the user directory jill is

```
/home/jill
```

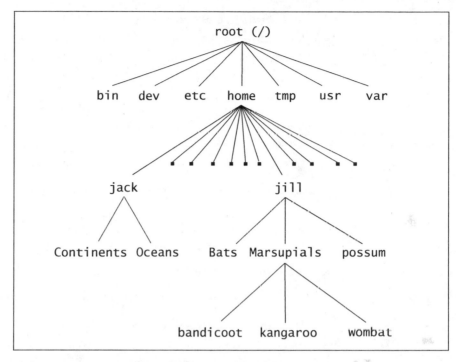

Figure 6-2
The home directories
jack and jill. A large
UNIX system may con-
tain hundreds of home
directories.

This is called the *pathname* of jill because it tells what path to follow to get from
the root directory to jill. In this case, the path goes from the root, to the
directory home, and finally to jill. Continuing further, the subdirectory
Marsupials has the absolute pathname

/home/jill/Marsupials

Ordinary files also have absolute pathnames. For example, the pathname of the file
wombat is

/home/jill/Marsupials/wombat

This means that wombat may be found by starting at the root, moving down to the
directory home, then to the user directory jill, to the directory Marsupials,
and finally to the file wombat itself.

You may have noticed that the slash (/) serves two purposes in pathnames. The
first slash represents the root; other slashes stand as separators between file names.

As you can imagine, a full pathname can be unwieldy. Fortunately, you can
abbreviate some pathnames. A tilde (~) by itself stands for your home directory's
pathname; a tilde preceding a user name stands for that user's home directory.
Thus,

~ represents the absolute pathname of your home directory

~jack represents the absolute pathname of the home directory jack

6.7 Relative Pathnames

A relative pathname shows
how to find a file, beginning
at your working directory.

More often than not, you are interested in the position of a file or directory relative to your current working directory. Relative pathnames start from the working directory rather than the root.

When writing out a relative pathname, a single period or dot (.) is the shorthand notation for your current working directory. Similarly, two dots (..) are used to signify the parent of your working directory—the one above it in the directory structure. These are usually called "dot" and "dotdot." Hence

Both "dot" and "dotdot" are
links—see Section 6.14.

. ("dot") represents the current working directory

.. ("dotdot") is the parent of the current working directory

For files in the current directory, the relative pathname is easy: it is simply the name of the file. Suppose you were working in the directory jack shown in Figure 6–2. The relative pathnames of the two directories in jack would be

```
Continents  Oceans
```

The parent of jack is home. Therefore, the relative pathname of home would be

```
..
```

Suppose now that you wanted the relative pathname of the directory that contains home, which is the root directory. From the directory jack this would be

```
../..
```

To find the Marsupials directory from the directory jack, you would first move up to home (represented by "dotdot"), then down to jill, and finally down to Marsupials itself. Putting this altogether, the relative pathname becomes

```
../jill/Marsupials
```

While absolute pathnames always begin with a slash (/), representing the root directory, relative pathnames begin either with "dot" (.), "dotdot" (..), or the name of a file or directory in your current working directory.

6.8 Listing Files

You now know how to write absolute pathnames and relative pathnames, but you may reasonably wonder what good this is. To answer that, consider how pathnames may be used with a few UNIX commands. Start with the ls ("list") command.

Suppose jack is working in his home directory, and he wants to remind himself which files he has in his home directory. He would type the command

§ ls (RETURN)

The response would be

```
Continents  Oceans
```

Now suppose jack wants to know what jill has in her Marsupials directory. From his home directory, he would use the ls command with the pathname of Marsupials:

§ ls ../jill/Marsupials (RETURN)

The computer's answer would be

```
bandicoot  kangaroo  wombat
```

Thus, without leaving home, jack can list files in a distant directory—even a directory belonging to another user—if he knows the directory's pathname.

6.9 Hidden Files and Directories

A *hidden* (or *invisible*) file is one that is not listed when you use the simple ls command. A file or directory will be hidden if its name begins with a period. For example,

```
.hidden    .jim    .lost    .profile    .login    .  ..
```

would all be hidden—they would not be listed by the simple ls command. To list all of the files in a directory, including the hidden ones, requires the ls -a ("list all") command. Suppose, for example, that jack is working in his home directory, and he types

§ ls -a (RETURN)

He would see

```
.  ..  Continents  Oceans
```

Similarly, if jack were to use this command with the pathname of jill's Marsupials directory, he would see something like this:

§ ls -a ../jill/Marsupials (RETURN)

```
.  ..  bandicoot  kangaroo  wombat
```

Note that "dot" (.) and "dotdot" (..) are both names of hidden directories, and that both appear when jack uses the ls -a command. Remember, "dot" is just another name for the current directory; "dotdot" refers to the parent of the current directory.

6.10 Renaming and Moving Files

The ls command takes one pathname; now consider a command that uses two. The mv ("move") command has the general form

mv *pathname1 pathname2*

This means "move the file found at *pathname1* to the position specified by *pathname2*." To see how this works, consider how jill might tidy up her home directory using mv.

The file name possum is wrong because the proper name for the animal is "opossum." If jill is still working in her home directory, the pathname of the file possum is just the file name. To change the name of the file without changing its location, she simply uses mv with the new name:

§ mv possum opossum (RETURN)

This means "move the contents of possum (in the current directory) into the file opossum (also in the current directory)." Since there is no existing opossum file, one is created, and the old file name disappears.

Next, jill remembers that the opossum is a marsupial, and therefore should be moved to the Marsupials directory. The mv command will do the trick:

§ mv opossum Marsupials (RETURN)

This means "move opossum from the current directory into the Marsupials directory." Thus jill can use the mv command twice, once to rename a file and again to move it to another directory. The end result is shown in Figure 6–3.

jill could have moved the file and renamed it at the same time using the command

§ mv possum Marsupials/opossum (RETURN)

This means "move the contents of possum to the Marsupials directory and into a file named opossum."

WARNING	BE CAREFUL WHEN MOVING OR RENAMING A FILE. IF A FILE HAVING THE SAME PATHNAME ALREADY EXISTS, THE EXISTING FILE WILL BE OVERWRITTEN.

6.11 Creating a File

There are four common ways to create a UNIX file:

1. Copy an existing file.

2. Redirect the "standard output" from a UNIX utility.

3. Use a text editor.

4. Write a computer program that opens new files.

Of these, (1) and (2) are considered in this chapter; (3) is covered later in the book. (Consult a book on your favorite programming language to see how to write a program that creates files.)

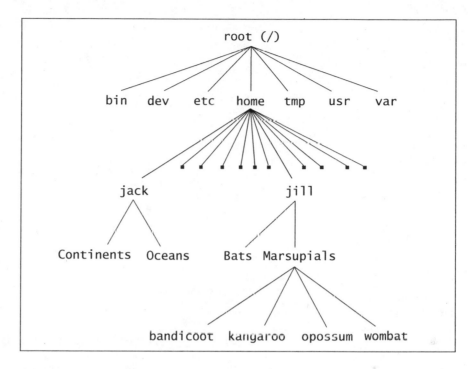

Figure 6-3
The home directory after the file pos sum was re-named opossum, then moved to the Marsupi-als directory.

6.12 Copying Files

The cp ("copy") command has the form

cp *pathname1 pathname2*

This means "copy the file found at *pathname1* and place the copy in the position specified by *pathname2*." Suppose that jack has developed a sudden interest in wombats and asks jill for a copy of her file on the subject. From her home directory, jill uses the command

§ cp Marsupials/wombat ../jack/Continents (RETURN)

to make a copy of the wombat file and put it in the Continents directory. The result is shown in Figure 6–4.

WARNING	BE CAREFUL WHEN NAMING A COPY. IF A FILE HAVING THE SAME PATHNAME ALREADY EXISTS, ITS CONTENTS WILL BE OVERWRITTEN.

6.13 Creating a File by Redirection

Redirection puts the output into a file rather than the terminal screen.

The second method of creating a new file is to redirect the output of a command. In other words, instead of displaying the results of the command on the screen, UNIX puts the results into a file. As an example, consider what happens if jill moves to her Marsupials directory and issues the ls command:

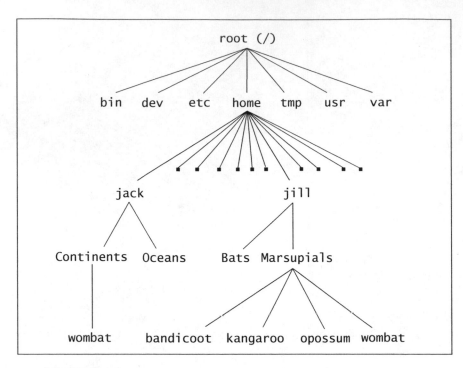

Figure 6-4
The home directory
after jill places a copy
of wombat in Conti-
nents.

§ ls (RETURN)
bandicoot kangaroo opossum wombat

Think of the redirection
symbol (>) as an arrow
pointing to the file where
the output should go.

Suppose now that she wants to redirect this list into a file named filelist. She does this using the *output redirection symbol* (>):

§ ls > filelist (RETURN)
§

Usually, the standard
output is the terminal
screen, and the standard
input is the keyboard.

This time, nothing appears on the screen because the output was rerouted into the file. In UNIX terminology, the information was redirected from the *standard output* (the terminal screen) to the file. If jill lists her files now, she will see that there is a new one named filelist in the directory:

§ ls (RETURN)
bandicoot filelist kangaroo opossum wombat

Redirection is powerful and convenient, but it can be dangerous. If you redirect the output into a file that already exists, the original contents of the file will be lost.

WARNING	REDIRECTION INTO AN EXISTING FILE WILL OVERWRITE WHATEVER IS ALREADY IN THE FILE.

If you want to add something to the end of an existing file while keeping the original contents, you can use the *append* operation. This requires two redirection symbols (>>):

Appending adds the output
to the end of the file.

```
§ ls >> filelist (RETURN)
§
```

6.14 Links

Although we have been saying that directory files contain other files and directories, that is not precisely true. If you could look inside a directory, you would find no files. Instead, you would see a list of the files that are supposed to be "contained" in that directory. The names on the list refer to the storage locations that actually hold the files. We say that the files are "linked" to the directory.

Generally, a *link* is a name that refers to a file. UNIX allows more than one link to the same file, so a file can have more than one name.

Directory files always contain at least two links: "dot" (.), which is a link to the directory itself; and "dotdot" (..), a link to the parent directory. Most ordinary files are created with just one link.

You can create more links to a file using the ln ("link") command:

```
§ ln filename newfilename (RETURN)
```

where *filename* is the name of an existing file, and *newfilename* is the new name you want to link to the file.

6.15 The Long Listing

The UNIX operating system is designed to make it easy for users to share files. However, there are times when you do not want others to copy, move, or even examine the contents of your files and directories. You can easily control access to the files in your home directory.

The ls -l ("list –long") command shows the current access permissions on a file or directory:

```
§ ls -l (RETURN)
```

This produces listings that look something like this:

```
drwxrwx---  2 you engr    12 Apr  1 15:53 Cal
-rw-rw----  1 you engr   997 Mar 31 10:53 fun
-rw-rw----  1 you engr   401 Mar 31 10:30 summer.2007
```

Let's decipher the first listing:

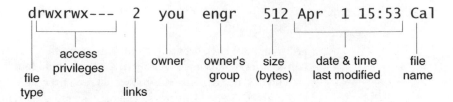

■ *File type.* A *d* in the leftmost position indicates a directory. An ordinary file will have a hyphen (–) in this position.

Access privileges are discussed in Section 6.16

■ *Access privileges.* These nine positions show who has permission to do what with the file or directory. (More will be said about these later.)

■ *Links.* Remember, a *link* is a pseudonym for a file or directory. Directory files always have at least two links, because each directory contains the hidden entry "dot" (.) as a pseudonym for itself and "dotdot" (..) as a pseudonym for the parent directory. Most ordinary files have just one link, but you can create more using the `ln` command.

■ *Owner.* This is the login of the person who owns the file.

■ *Owner's group.* A *group* is a collection of users to which the owner of the file belongs. (On Berkeley systems, `ls -l` does not list the group name; to see it, you have to use the `ls -lg` command.)

■ *Size.* The size of the file is given in bytes.

■ *Date and time.* The date and time the file was last modified is shown here.

■ *File name.* The name of the file or directory is listed last.

6.16 Access Privileges

In the previous section, we saw how the `ls -l` ("list –long") command can be used to get information on a file, including the access privileges. The nine entries showing the access permissions deserve a closer look:

`rwxrwx---`

Basically, there are three things that can be done to an ordinary file:

r   *Read.* Examine (but not change) the contents of the file.

w   *Write.* Change the contents of a file.

x   *Execute.* If the file contains a program, run that program.

Likewise, there are three things that can be done to a directory:

r   *Read.* List the contents of the directory using the `ls` command.

w   *Write.* Change the contents of the directory by creating new files or removing existing files. (To edit an existing file requires write permission on that file.)

x   *Execute.* "Search" the directory using `ls -l`. Also, move to the directory from another directory, and copy files from the directory.

When deciding who can have access to a file, UNIX recognizes three categories of users:

■ *Owner.* The owner of the file or directory.

■ *Group.* Other users belonging to the user's group.

■ *Public.* All other users on the system.

The first three permissions show what the owner may do; the next three show what the group may do; the last three show what the public may do. For example,

rwxrwx---   owner has read, write, and execute privileges

group has read, write, and execute privileges

public has no privileges

rw-rw----   owner has read and write privileges

group has read and write privileges

public has no privileges

r--r--r--   owner has read privileges only

group has read privileges only

public has read privileges only

6.17 Changing File Modes

The access privileges are sometimes called the *mode* of the file or directory. To change the mode, you use the `chmod` ("change mode") command. `chmod` uses the following notation:

u   user (owner) of the file

g   group

o   others (public)

a   all (owner, group, and public)

–   assign a permission

+   add a permission

–   remove a permission

A few examples will help you see how chmod is used. To give the owner execute permission without changing any other permissions, you would use

§ chmod u+x *filename* (RETURN)

Note that there are no spaces between u and +, or between + and x.

To remove read and write permissions from group members, you would use

§ chmod g-rw *filename* (RETURN)

The following command will give everyone read permissions while removing any other permissions:

§ chmod a=r *filename* (RETURN)

To give the user read and write permissions and everyone else read privileges, use

Do not put space(s) after the comma.

§ chmod u=rw,go=r *filename* (RETURN)

6.18 Exercises

1. What are the rules for naming UNIX files and directories?

2. Which of the following would be valid names for ordinary UNIX files? Explain.

foo	guess?	book.chap1	BOOK.chap2
2good2Btrue	{2bad}	>right>	<left<
name	rank*	serial#	^up^
el_paso	w.lafayette	New York	/slash\
.hideNseek	.357	747	passwd

3. Which of the following would be valid directory names? Explain.

doo_wa	dir1	Dir2	Directory.3
*Hook	|Line|	"Sinker"	money.$
Game	Set	Match	sticks
[Groucho]	'Chico'	Harpo.#	Karl?
.hideNseek	.357	747	passwd

Exercises 4 through 11 refer to the hypothetical UNIX file system previously shown in Figure 6–4. (Hint: It may be helpful to sketch the directory structure as you go along.) These exercises should be done in order.

4. What are the absolute pathnames for root, bin, jill, and kangaroo?

5. Suppose that Marsupials is now your working directory. What are the relative pathnames of root, bin, jill, and kangaroo?

6. jack has two subdirectories, Continents and Oceans.

a. What are the absolute pathnames of Continents and Oceans?

b. From Oceans, what are the relative pathnames of root, etc, and bandicoot?

7. Imagine that jack sets up additional subdirectories to hold geographical information. Continents contains Africa, Antarctica, Asia, Australia, Europe, NAmerica, and SAmerica. Each of these directories contains subdirectories for individual countries or regions. For example, NAmerica contains the subdirectories Canada, CentralAm, Mexico, and USA. Assuming every file and directory to be in its proper place, give the absolute pathnames of the following directories:

a. Norway;

b. India;

c. Egypt;

d. Argentina.

8. Suppose jack's working directory is USA. Show how he could accomplish the following tasks, *using a single command line and relative pathnames in each case*:

a. List the contents of the Marsupials directory belonging to jill.

b. List the contents of Australia.

c. Make a copy of jill's file kangaroo, and place it under the name kangaroo in his Australia directory.

9. Repeat the previous problem using absolute pathnames.

10. The directory Canada has twelve subdirectories, one for each of the ten provinces and two territories. Suppose jack's working directory is SAmerica. Show how he could accomplish the following tasks, *using a single command line and relative pathnames in each case*:

a. List the contents of BC, the directory for British Columbia, Canada.

b. Place a copy of the file for Vancouver, British Columbia, in the directory jill.

11. Repeat the previous problem using absolute pathnames.

12. Suppose you have a file named stuff in your working directory. Specify the command(s) you would use to do the following:

a. Give everyone permission to read stuff; do not change any other privileges.

b. Permit the owner and group members to read and write the file; remove all privileges from everyone else.

c. Remove writing privileges from everyone but the owner.

d. Give the owner and group members permission to execute stuff while giving the owner sole permission to read or write it.

13. Suppose you have a directory named MyStuff in your working directory. Specify the command(s) you would use to do the following:

a. Give everyone permission to list files in MyStuff; do not change any other privileges.

b. Permit the owner and group members to list, remove, or add files; remove all privileges from everyone else.

c. Remove writing privileges from everyone but the owner.

d. Give the owner and group members permission to execute MyStuff while giving the owner sole permission to read or write it.

Tutorial:
Working with Files

In this chapter, you will learn how to create, view, copy, rename, and print files. All of your work will take place in your home directory—you'll see how to make subdirectories in the next chapter.

7.1 Printing a Calendar

Many of the examples in this chapter make use of the UNIX utility `cal`, which displays a calendar for any month or any year from AD 1 to AD 9999. To see how this works, try some examples:

1. Print a calendar for a given month. For example, to show the calendar for the twelfth month of the year 2007, type the command

§ `cal 12 2007` (RETURN)

The computer will respond with the calendar:

```
   December 2007
 S  M Tu  W Th  F  S
                   1
 2  3  4  5  6  7  8
 9 10 11 12 13 14 15
16 17 18 19 20 21 22
23 24 25 26 27 28 29
30 31
```

2. Print a calendar for an entire year. To do this, specify the year but not the month:

§ `cal 2007` (RETURN)

A calendar for the year 2007 should have appeared on your screen, although it probably scrolled by too fast for you to read it all. Don't worry; in a moment you will see how to save this calendar in a file that you can examine at your leisure.

7.2   Creating a File by Redirection

Many UNIX commands print their output on the standard output, usually the computer screen. However, the UNIX shell allows you to redirect the output into a file. Let's do this using the `cal` command.

The rules for naming UNIX files are given in Section 6.5.

1. Select a name for the file. Remember to use descriptive file names. An appropriate name for a file holding the calendar for the year 2007 would be 2007.

2. Enter the `cal` command, followed by the redirection operator (>) and the file name. To put the calendar for the year 2007 into the file 2007, type

Think of > as an arrow pointing where the output will go.

§ `cal 2007 > 2007` (RETURN)

This time, the calendar does not appear on the screen; instead, the standard output from `cal` has been redirected into the file 2007.

The UNIX shell does not tell you when it has successfully created a file by redirection.

3. List the file names in your current working directory. How do you know if the new file was created? You can check this by listing the files in your working directory using the `ls` command:

§ `ls` (RETURN)

The name of the new file should appear:

2007

Redirection created a file named 2007 in your home directory. Had there already been a file named 2007, its contents would have been replaced.

WARNING	REDIRECTION INTO AN EXISTING FILE WILL OVERWRITE WHATEVER IS ALREADY IN THE FILE.

7.3   Viewing a File with cat

Catenate means "join together," which is one of the functions of `cat`.

Suppose you want to see the **contents** of a file, not just its name. One way to do this is by the use of the `cat` ("catenate") command.

■ **Type `cat`, followed by the file name.** Thus, to look at the 2007 file, type

§ `cat 2007` (RETURN)

This displays the file, but it scrolls by so fast that the first few lines cannot be read. Fortunately, UNIX provides a more convenient means of viewing files.

7.4   Viewing with more

The `more` command allows you to display a file, one screen at a time.

1. Enter the `more` command and the file name. To view the file 2007, type the command line

§ `more 2007` (RETURN)

This will display as much of the file as will fit on the screen at one time. If the entire file does not fit, a message will appear in the lower corner of the screen, telling you that more remains to be seen:

```
--More--
```

2. To see more of the file, press the space bar. This will show you the next screenful.

3. To exit without viewing the entire file, type q or Q (for quit). It is not necessary to press (RETURN):

```
q
```

You will know that you are out of the more program when you see the UNIX shell prompt:

```
§
```

7.5   Viewing with pg

Some UNIX systems offer the pg ("page") command as an alternative to more.

1. Enter the pg command and the file name. To view the file 2007, type the command line

```
§ pg  2007 (RETURN)
```

This will display as much of the file as will fit on the screen at one time. If the entire file does not fit, a colon (:) appears at the bottom of the screen to indicate that more of the file remains to be seen.

```
:
```

2. To see more, press (RETURN). This will show you the next screenful of the file.

3. To exit without viewing the whole file, type q or Q (for quit). It is not necessary to press (RETURN):

```
q
```

You will know that you are out of the pg program when you see the UNIX shell prompt:

```
§
```

7.6   Chaining Files Together with cat

You previously used the cat command to view the contents of a file. When given a single file name, cat simply displays the contents of that file; when two or more file names are used together, cat displays all of the files, one after another. This can be used to join together the contents of multiple files.

Your next task is to use cat to make a calendar for the summer months of 2007. First, use the cal utility to make three files:

§ cal 6 2007 > jun.2007 (RETURN)
§ cal 7 2007 > jul.2007 (RETURN)
§ cal 8 2007 > aug.2007 (RETURN)

1. View the files with cat. Enter the cat command followed by the file names:

§ cat jun.2007 jul.2007 aug.2007 (RETURN)

The contents of the files will be displayed, one right after another:

```
    June 2007
 S  M Tu  W Th  F  S
             1  2
 3  4  5  6  7  8  9
10 11 12 13 14 15 16
17 18 19 20 21 22 23
24 25 26 27 28 29 30
    July 2007
 S  M Tu  W Th  F  S
 1  2  3  4  5  6  7
 8  9 10 11 12 13 14
15 16 17 18 19 20 21
22 23 24 25 26 27 28
29 30 31
   August 2007
 S  M Tu  W Th  F  S
          1  2  3  4
 5  6  7  8  9 10 11
12 13 14 15 16 17 18
19 20 21 22 23 24 25
26 27 28 29 30 31
```

2. Use cat again, but redirect the output into another file. For example, to create a file named summer.2007, enter the command

§ cat jun.2007 jul.2007 aug.2007 > summer.2007 (RETURN)

This creates a new file containing a three-month calendar. Note that the redirection operator is required here.

3. List the files.

§ ls (RETURN)

The new file should appear:

```
2007  aug.2007  jul.2007  jun.2007  summer.2007
```

7.7   Appending to a File

The UNIX shell allows you to add information to the end of an existing file, an operation called *appending*.

■ **Type the command, the append operator, and the name of the file.** To append the calendar for September 2007 to the file summer.2007, type the following line, making sure to use the append symbol (>>):

§ cal 9 2007 >> summer.2007 (RETURN)

Had you used the regular redirection symbol (>), the calendar for September would have replaced the calendars for June, July, and August that were already in the file. Instead, the September calendar was added to the end of the summer.2007 file.

7.8   Copying a File with cp

The cp ("copy") command is used to copy files. We will use it to make a copy of the file summer.2007.

1. Think of a name for the copy. The usual rules for naming UNIX files apply. An appropriate name for a file containing a calendar for the summer of 2007 might be SUMM.2007.

WARNING	BE CAREFUL WHEN NAMING A COPY. IF A FILE HAVING THE SAME PATHNAME ALREADY EXISTS, ITS CONTENTS WILL BE OVERWRITTEN.

2. Enter the cp command, followed by the names of the original file and the copy. To make a copy of summer.2007 named SUMM.2007, type

This means "copy summer.2007 into SUMM.2007."

§ cp summer.2007 SUMM.2007 (RETURN)

In this case, there is no existing file with the name SUMM.2007, so one is created.

3. Verify that the new file appears. UNIX does not alert you that a file has been copied, so you will have to check this yourself using the ls command:

§ ls (RETURN)

The computer will list all of the files in the current directory, including the new file:

2007   SUMM.2007   aug.2007   jul.2007   jun.2007   summer.2007

There is just one small problem with this example: the convention in this book is to use lowercase letters for file names, and to capitalize directory names. (You don't have to do this, but it helps distinguish files from directories.) SUMM.2007 is an ordinary file, not a directory, so in the next section you will give it a different name.

7.9   Renaming a File with mv

The mv ("move") command is used for renaming files. (It is also used for moving files to other directories, as you will see in the next chapter.)

1. Choose a new name for the file. As usual, you should choose names that are short and descriptive. An appropriate name for a file containing a calendar for the summer of 2007 might be vacation.2007.

WARNING	BE CAREFUL WHEN RENAMING A FILE. IF A FILE HAVING THE SAME PATHNAME ALREADY EXISTS, THE EXISTING FILE WILL BE OVERWRITTEN.

2. Enter the mv command, followed by the old name and the new name. To rename SUMM.2007 as vacation.2007, type the command line

§ mv SUMM.2007 vacation.2007 (RETURN)

3. Verify that the new file name appears in the directory. Because UNIX does not tell you that the file has been renamed, you will have to check this yourself using the ls command:

§ ls (RETURN)

The computer will list all of the files in the current directory:

2007 aug.2007 jul.2007 jun.2007 summer.2007 vacation.2007

The difference between cp (copy) and mv (move) is that cp creates a new file, leaving the old file intact, while mv simply renames the old file.

7.10   Printing on the Default Printer

Frequently, you are likely to require hardcopy output from your files. How you produce this depends on the number and type of printers available to you, as well as the type of UNIX you are using.

■ **Enter the simple line printer command, followed by the file name.** If you are using Berkeley UNIX, enter the lpr ("line printer") command:

§ lpr 2007 (RETURN)

On AT&T UNIX, enter the lp command:

§ lp 2007 (RETURN)

7.11 Printing on Other Printers

If your computer system has more than one printer attached to it, the simple line printer command used in the previous section will send your files to the default printer. You can specify another printer with the -P or -d option. To do this, you first have to know the code for the printer you are to use; ask your instructor, consultant, or system administrator.

■ **Enter the line printer command and specify the printer and the file to be printed.** On Berkeley UNIX you would type the following command, making sure to insert the proper printer code in place of *code*:

§ lpr -P*code* 2007 (RETURN)

Note that there is a space before the -P and before the file name, but not between the -P and the printer code.

On AT&T UNIX, you would type the following command, inserting the printer code in place of *code*:

§ lp -d*code* 2007 (RETURN)

Here again, there is a space before -d and before the file name, but not between the -d and the printer code.

7.12 Removing Unneeded Files

When a file is no longer useful, you should remove it so that it won't take up valuable storage space. This is done with the rm ("remove") command, which takes the pathname of the file to be removed. Since you probably don't need two copies of the summer 2007 calendar, remove one of them.

1. Use the ls command to check the file name. Since on many systems you cannot retrieve a file once it has been removed, it is a good idea to be sure of the file name:

§ ls (RETURN)

2007 aug.2007 jul.2007 jun.2007 summer.2007 vacation.2007

2. Type rm, followed by the file's pathname. To remove vacation.2007, type the command line

§ rm vacation.2007 (RETURN)

3. Verify that the file is gone. UNIX does not tell you that the file has been removed, so you will have to check this yourself using the ls command:

§ ls (RETURN)

2007 aug.2007 jul.2007 jun.2007 summer.2007

7.13 Command Summary

Each command is typed in after the UNIX shell prompt, and each is terminated by a (RETURN). Note that *file*, *file1*, and *file2* may be simple file names or pathnames.

Making Calendars

cal *m year*	show a calendar for month *m* (1-12) of *year* (1–9999)
cal *year*	show a calendar for *year*
cal *year* > *file*	redirect calendar for *year* into *file*
cal *year* >> *file*	append calendar for *year* to *file*

Listing and Viewing Files

ls	list files in working directory
cat *file*	show contents of *file* all at once
more *file*	show contents of *file* one screen at a time; press spacebar to continue or q to quit
pg *file*	Like more. Press (RETURN) to see next screen, q to quit

Printing Files

lpr *file*	send *file* to default line printer (BSD UNIX)
lp *file*	send *file* to default line printer (AT&T UNIX)
lpr –P*code* *file*	send *file* to printer designated by *code* (BSD)
lp –d*code* *file*	send *file* to printer designated by *code* (AT&T)

Copying, Renaming, and Removing Files

cp *file1* *file2*	copy *file1* into *file2*; retain both copies of the file
mv *file1* *file2*	move (i.e., rename) *file1* to *file2*; retain only *file2*
rm *file*	remove (i.e., delete) *file*

7.14 Exercises

1. What are the rules for selecting UNIX file names?

2. Because of the need to make certain adjustments to the calendar, the month of September 1752 was a very unusual one. What was different about it?

3. The echo command takes a line that you type in and repeats it back on the screen. Thus if you type

```
echo This is fun! (RETURN)
```

The computer will respond with

```
This is fun!
```

Redirect this phrase into a file named fun.

4. Using the commands who, who am i, and date, append to the fun file (see Exercise 3 above) a list of the users currently logged onto the computer, your login, and the current date.

5. A hidden file has a name that begins with a period (.). Use the cal utility and the redirection operator (>) to create a file named .hidden, then use ls to list your files. Do you see the .hidden file? Now try the ls -a command. Does .hidden appear? What other hidden file entries do you see?

6. Many UNIX systems offer a utility named file, which classifies files according to their contents. The utility examines the file and tries to determine what kind of information it may contain. Some of the classifications used by file are

ascii text	c program text	commands
data	directory	empty
English text	executable	

Try out the file command on the files and directories in your system. Does file always classify files correctly?

Chapter 8

TUTORIAL: WORKING WITH DIRECTORIES

A directory is a file that contains other files and directories. In this chapter, you will see how to create directories, move files between directories, rename files, and delete directories you no longer need.

8.1 Your Directory Structure Thus Far

If you have carefully followed the examples in the text and worked through all of the end-of-chapter exercises, your file system should resemble the structure shown in Figure 8–1. At this point, your home directory contains no subdirectories. You are now ready to create new subdirectories inside your home directory.

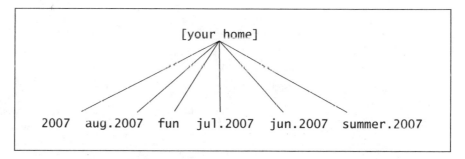

Figure 8-1
Your file system after completing the previous chapter.

8.2 Creating a Subdirectory

It's time to make a directory to hold the calendars you made in the previous chapter. For this we use the `mkdir` ("make directory") command.

Note that the directory name `Cal` differs from the `cal` command—remember, UNIX is case-sensitive.

1. Select an appropriate name for the new directory. The rules for naming directories are the same as for files. (However, in this book we will capitalize the names of any new directories we create to distinguish them from ordinary files.) A descriptive name for a directory to hold calendars would be `Cal`.

2. Enter `mkdir` followed by the new directory name. Remember to capitalize the directory name:

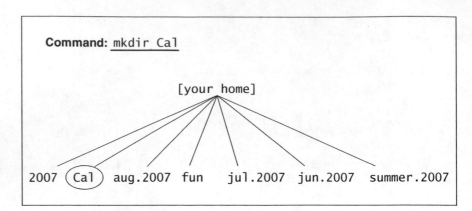

Command: `mkdir Cal`

[your home]

2007 (Cal) aug.2007 fun jul.2007 jun.2007 summer.2007

Figure 8-2
Your file system after creating the subdirectory Cal. At this point, Cal contains no files.

§ `mkdir Cal` (RETURN)

3. Use the `ls` command to see that the new directory exists:

§ `ls` (RETURN)

The new directory name should appear, along with the names of the files you made before:

`2007  Cal  aug.2007  fun  jul.2007  jun.2007  summer.2007`

(If you have been following the examples in the text, your file system should resemble Figure 8–2.)

8.3 Moving Files between Directories

Recall that you previously used `mv` to rename a file.

When a new subdirectory is first created, it contains no files. In this section, you will see how to move a file to a new subdirectory using the `mv` ("move") command, which you previously used to rename files.

1. Type the `mv` command, the file's name, and the destination directory's name. To put 2007 into the directory Cal, enter the command line

§ `mv 2007 Cal` (RETURN)

This puts 2007 inside Cal (see Figure 8–3).

2. List the files in your home directory. Check to see that 2007 has indeed been moved:

§ `ls` (RETURN)

The 2007 file will not appear because it is now inside the Cal subdirectory:

`Cal aug.2007 fun jul.2007 jun.2007 summer.2007`

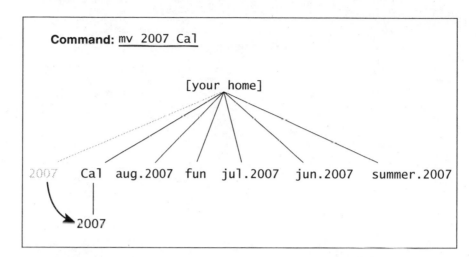

Figure 8-3
Moving the file 2007
into Cal.

8.4 Creating Directories Using Pathnames

Your next task is to create a subdirectory inside Cal to hold monthly calendars. A good, descriptive name for this directory is Months. Since this is to go inside Cal, the pathname of the new directory relative to your home directory will be Cal/Months.

■ **Enter the mkdir command, followed by the pathname of the new directory.**
Thus, to create a directory Months inside the directory Cal, type

Remember to capitalize
Months to emphasize that
it is a directory name.

§ mkdir Cal/Months (RETURN)

With the creation of Months, your directory structure should resemble the one shown in Figure 8-4.

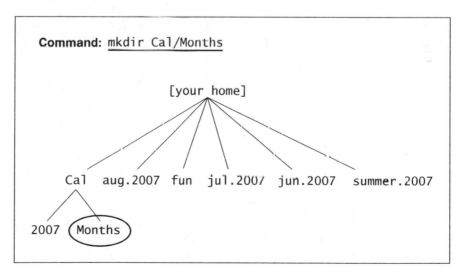

Figure 8-4
Directory structure after
creation of the subdirec-
tory Months.

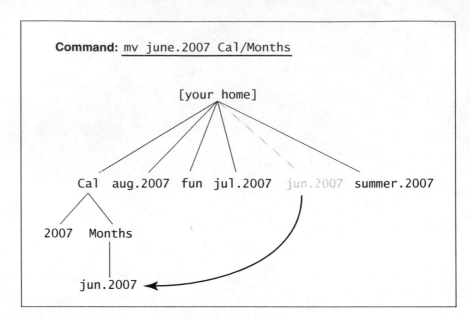

Figure 8-5
Directory structure after
moving jun.2007 into
the subdirectory
Months.

8.5   Using Pathnames to Move Files

In this section, you will move a file into the Months directory, using a pathname to specify the file's new location.

1.   Enter the mv command, the file name, and the new pathname. Thus, to move the file jun.2007 into Months, type

§ mv jun.2007 Cal/Months (RETURN)

At this point, your directory structure should look something like Figure 8–5.

2.   List the files in the current directory. The ls command should show that jun.2007 is no longer in the current directory:

§ ls (RETURN)
Cal aug.2007 fun jul.2007 summer.2007

8.6   Using Pathnames to Move and Rename Files

In this section, you will move a file and rename it with one command, using a pathname to specify both the file's new location and its new name.

■ **Enter the mv command, the file name, and the new pathname.** To move the file aug.2007 into Months, and rename it 08.2007, type

§ mv aug.2007 Cal/Months/08.2007 (RETURN)

The result of this operation is shown in Figure 8–6.

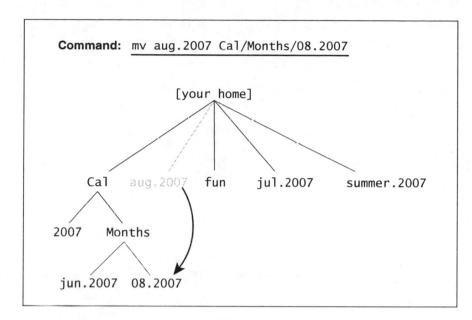

Command: mv aug.2007 Cal/Months/08.2007

[your home]

Cal   aug.2007   fun   jul.2007   summer.2007

2007   Months

jun.2007   08.2007

Figure 8-6
Moving and renaming
aug.2007.

8.7 Working in a Distant Directory

As you have seen, the simple ls command only lists files and directories in the current working directory. To list files in another directory, you must give ls that directory's pathname. As you will see in this section, you can work with the files in the directory Months without leaving your home directory.

1. Enter the list command, followed by the pathname of the directory you wish to examine. Thus, to see the contents of Months, type:

§ ls Cal/Months (RETURN)

You should see

08.2007   jun.2007

2. Enter the cat command, followed by the pathname of the file you want to view. You can view the contents of the file 08.2007 from your home directory using the cat command with the appropriate pathname:

§ cat Cal/Months/08.2007 (RETURN)

The contents of 08.2007 will appear on the screen:

```
    August 2007
 S  M Tu  W Th  F  S
             1  2  3  4
 5  6  7  8  9 10 11
12 13 14 15 16 17 18
19 20 21 22 23 24 25
26 27 28 29 30 31
```

8.8   Changing Your Working Directory

You can change your current working directory using the cd ("change directory")
command with the pathname of the target directory.

■ **Enter the cd command followed by the pathname of the target directory.**
Thus, to move to the subdirectory Months, type

§ cd Cal/Months (RETURN)

This makes Months your working directory.

8.9   Returning to Your Home Directory

To return to your home directory, you **could** use cd with either the absolute or the
relative pathname of your home directory. However, there is a much easier way.

■ **Enter the cd command without a pathname.** This will always get you back to
your home directory, regardless of where you are in the file structure:

§ cd (RETURN)

8.10   Printing Your Working Directory

As you might imagine, it is easy to get lost among the hundreds of directories in a
large UNIX system. The pwd ("print working directory") command always
displays the absolute pathname of your current working directory.

■ **Type pwd.** This will print your location relative to the root:

§ pwd (RETURN)

8.11   Removing Directories

A directory that is no longer needed may be removed using the rmdir ("remove
directory") command. You cannot remove a directory unless it is first emptied of
files and other directories. This is a safety feature, intended to prevent you from
accidentally throwing away files that you meant to keep.

1. **Enter the rmdir command, followed by the pathname of the directory.** To
remove the subdirectory Cal, type

§ rmdir Cal (RETURN)

If the directory contains files, the shell will respond with a message such as

rmdir: Cal: Directory not empty

2. **If necessary, use rm to remove any files in the directory.** Then repeat step 1.
Because you will need the Cal directory to complete the exercises, do not remove
it yet.

8.12 Command Summary

Each of these commands is typed in after the UNIX prompt, and each is terminated by a $\boxed{\text{RETURN}}$. *Dir* and *file* represent the pathnames of a directory and a file, respectively.

mkdir *Dir*	make a directory having the pathname *Dir*
mv *file Dir*	move *file* into the directory *Dir*
cd *Dir*	change to directory having the pathname *Dir*
cd	change to home directory
rmdir *Dir*	remove (i.e., delete) the directory *Dir*
pwd	print working directory's pathname

8.13 Exercises

1. What are the rules for naming UNIX directories?

2. What is the absolute pathname of your home directory?

3. Create a new directory Misc and move the file fun inside this new directory.

4. Without leaving your home directory, create a directory named Vacations inside Cal. Then move summer.2007 into this new directory.

5. Prepare a sketch of your directory structure after completing Exercises 2 through 4 above.

10.2   Your Login Shell

When your UNIX account was created, the system administrator selected a shell for you. This is called your *login shell*, because it is the shell you use each time you log in.

Once you have worked with the various shells available on your system, you may decide to change your login shell. On some systems, you can do this yourself using the chsh ("change shell") command; on others, the system administrator must make the change for you.

10.3   How the Shell Processes Commands

The entire process can be summarized this way:

1. The shell displays a prompt symbol on the screen. The prompt tells you the shell is ready to receive your commands.

2. You type in a command. As you type, the shell stores the characters and also echoes them back to the terminal screen.

3. You type (RETURN). This is the signal for the shell to interpret the command and start working on it.

4. The shell interprets your command. In most cases, the shell looks for the appropriate software to run your command. If the shell can't find the right software, it gives you an error message; otherwise, the shell asks the kernel to run it.

5. The kernel runs the requested software. While the command is running, the shell "goes to sleep." When the kernel finishes, it "wakes up" the shell.

6. The shell displays a prompt symbol. This indicates that the shell is once again ready to receive your commands.

We will say more about the search path in Part VI.

How does the shell know where to find software to run (Step 4)? The answer is that the shell looks through a predetermined list of directories called the *search path*.

This is a good place to point out the difference between a program and a process in UNIX jargon. A *program* is a set of coded instructions contained in a file. An example of a program is the ls command: it is just a sequence of computer instructions contained in the file /bin/ls. Similarly, your login shell is also just another program residing in the directory /bin.

A process is a running program.

A *process* is what you get whenever the computer runs a program. Thus, when you issue the ls command, the computer creates an ls process by running the program in the file /bin/ls. Likewise, when you log in, the computer looks in the file containing the shell program and creates a shell process for you.

The important thing to remember is that there is only one copy of the ls program, but there may be many active ls processes. In the same way, there is only one copy of each shell program, but there may be many active shell processes.

UNIX SHELLS

Tutorials related to this
chapter are found in
Chapters 11 and 12.

The *shell* is the UNIX command processor. When you type a command and press (RETURN), it is the shell that interprets the command and takes the appropriate action. In this chapter, you will see how the shell works.

10.1 Common Shells

Although dozens of shells have been written for the UNIX operating system, only a handful are in widespread use. The UNIX shells discussed in this chapter can be grouped into two "families." The first is the Bourne Shell family:

■ **Bourne Shell** (sh). Written by Steven Bourne at AT&T's Bell Labs, sh was the first major UNIX shell. It has been a part of nearly every UNIX system since Version 7 was released in 1979.

■ **Korn Shell** (ksh). The Korn Shell was created by David Korn at AT&T as an improved Bourne Shell. The first version of ksh was released in 1986, with major upgrades in 1988 and 1993.

■ **Bourne Again Shell** (bash). Originally written by Brian Fox for the GNU project of the Free Software Foundation, bash was released publicly in 1988. Further development of bash has been carried on by Chet Ramey, who released Version 2.0 in 1996.

The second family of shells is the C Shell family:

■ **C Shell** (csh). The C Shell was written by Bill Joy (who also wrote the vi editor) at the University of California at Berkeley. This shell was included with BSD UNIX in 1979, and has been found on most subsequent UNIX systems.

■ **TC Shell** (tcsh). An improved version of the C Shell, the TC Shell was developed in the late 1970s and early 1980s by a number of programmers (most notably Ken Greer at Carnegie-Mellon University and Paul Placeway at Ohio State).

10.4 Options and Arguments

The typical UNIX command can take one or more options which modify what the command does. Table 10-1 shows some options for the `ls` ("list") command.

Most commands allow you to specify multiple options. Thus, to prepare a reversed long listing of all files in the directory *Dir*, flagging directories and executable files, you could type

Note that each option is preceded by a hyphen.

§ `ls -a -l -r -F` *Dir* (RETURN)

Or you could combine the options:

§ `ls -alrF` *Dir* (RETURN)

Incidentally, anything that follows the command name—including the options and file names—is generally referred to as an *argument*.

Table 10-1
Some options for the
`ls` ("list") command.

Command	Effect
`ls`	List files in the current directory (except hidden files)
`ls -a`	List all files in the current directory, including hidden files
`ls -F`	Flag the files: show a slash (/) after each directory and an asterisk (*) after each executable file
`ls -l`	Print "long" list of files (except hidden files)
`ls -r`	List files in reverse order
`ls -s`	List files by size
`ls -t`	List files by time of last modification
`ls -u`	List files by time of last access

10.5 Standard Input, Output, and Error

Whenever you run a UNIX command or other program, the operating system opens up three standard channels for input and output:

■ **Standard input.** The standard input (or `stdin`) is the file where the program normally looks for input.

■ **Standard output.** The standard output (`stdout`) is the file where the program sends output.

■ **Standard error.** The standard error (`stderr`) is the file where the program sends error messages.

Remember: to UNIX, everything is a file.

Although we have defined `stdin`, `stdout`, and `stderr` as files, keep in mind that a UNIX file is nearly *anything* that can send or receive data. Most of the time we use "standard input" to mean the keyboard, and both "standard output" and "standard error" to mean the terminal screen.

Much of the power of UNIX derives from the shell's ability to reroute the standard input/output channels. A UNIX program is typically designed so that its standard input can be the keyboard, an ordinary file, or another program. Likewise, its standard output and standard error can be the terminal screen, an ordinary file, or another program.

10.6 Redirection

As we have said, the "standard output" is usually the terminal screen. However, the shell allows you to redirect the standard output so that the output goes into an ordinary file instead. For example, you have already seen how to use the output redirection operator (>) to create a file containing a calendar:

§ `cal 2007 > calendar.file` (RETURN)

You can add output to a file using the append operator (>>):

§ `cal 2008 >> calendar.file` (RETURN)

It is also possible to redirect the standard input so that a process takes its input from an ordinary file rather than the keyboard. For example, the `mail` command allows you to send and read electronic mail. To send the contents of the file `my.message` to the user `jones`, you could enter the command line

§ `mail jones < my.message` (RETURN)

You can combine input and output redirection in the same command line. For example, the following command line invokes the `wc` utility to count the lines, words, and characters in the file `input`, then redirects the results into the file `output`:

§ `wc < input > output` (RETURN)

10.7 Grouping Commands

Normally you type one command at a time, following each command by a (RETURN), which is the signal for the shell to begin its work. However, it is possible to put multiple commands on the same line, if you separate the commands with semicolons. Thus the command line

§ `who; ls; cal` (RETURN)

has the same effect as the three separate command lines

§ `who` (RETURN)
§ `ls` (RETURN)
§ `cal` (RETURN)

Grouping commands can be especially useful when you want to redirect the output into a file. You could make a calendar for the summer of 2007 in three steps:

```
§ cal 6 2007 > summer.2007 (RETURN)
§ cal 7 2007 >> summer.2007 (RETURN)
§ cal 8 2007 >> summer.2007 (RETURN)
```

You could accomplish the same thing with just one line:

```
§ (cal 6 2007; cal 7 2007; cal 8 2007) > summer.2007 (RETURN)
```

Note the parentheses; these are necessary to make sure the calendars for June, July, and August are all redirected into the same file. Suppose you were to omit the parentheses, like this:

```
§ cal 6 2007; cal 7 2007; cal 8 2007 > summer.2007 (RETURN)
```

In this case, the calendars for June and July would appear on the screen, and only the August calendar would be redirected into the file.

10.8   Pipes

Suppose you wanted to display the calendars for the years 2007, 2008, and 2009, one right after the other. You could type the command line

```
§ cal 2007; cal 2008; cal 2009 (RETURN)
```

This will print the calendars on the standard output, but they will scroll by so fast that you cannot read them. One way around this problem is to redirect the output into a file:

```
§ (cal 2007; cal 2008; cal 2009) > temp (RETURN)
```

Now you can view the contents of temp using the more or pg utility:

```
§ more temp (RETURN)
```

or

```
§ pg temp (RETURN)
```

This will work, but it requires that you create a temporary file just to look at the output from the commands. You can avoid creating a file by using what is called a *pipe*, which connects the output from one utility to the input of another. A vertical bar (|) is the pipe symbol. You would pipe the output from command1 to command2 like this:

```
command1 | command2
```

Thus, to view the calendars for 2007, 2008, and 2009, we can pipe the output of the cal utility to either more or pg:

§ (cal 2007; cal 2008; cal 2009) | more (RETURN)

or

§ (cal 2007; cal 2008; cal 2009) | pg (RETURN)

Note how this differs from redirection with > or >>. Redirection places the output from a utility into an ordinary file; the piping operation directs the output to another utility.

10.9 Tees

A *tee* allows you to do two things at once: (1) save the output from a command in a file, and (2) pipe the output to another command. We could take the output from *command1* and send it to the file *outfile* and to *command2* like this:

command1 | tee *outfile* | *command2*

Thus the command line

§ (cal 2008; cal 2009) | tee calfile | more (RETURN)

places copies of the calendars for 2008 and 2009 into the file calfile as they are also displayed on the terminal screen by more.

10.10 Filters

A *filter* takes a stream of data from its standard input, transforms the data in some way, and sends the results to the standard output. Table 10-2 shows some of the filters commonly found on UNIX systems.

Filters are often used with pipes and tees. Consider the sort utility, which, as you might expect, sorts its input. Suppose you wanted to list, alphabetically by their login names, the users currently logged onto your machine. You could do this by piping the output from who into sort:

§ who | sort (RETURN)

You can also give sort the name of a file to sort:

sort is discussed in   § sort poems (RETURN)
Chapter 11.

This would sort the lines of the file poems alphabetically. By default, the sort utility puts blanks first, then uppercase letters, then lowercase letters. This order can be reversed using the -r option:

§ sort -r poems (RETURN)

The sort utility takes many other options, some of which are discussed in Chapter 11.

Filter	Function
cat	Catenate and display text
comm	Compare sorted files, selecting or rejecting lines common to both
crypt	Encode or decode text
cut	Cut out selected fields from input lines
diff	Display line-by-line differences between two files
egrep	Search text for a pattern using full regular expressions
fgrep	Search text for a character string
fmt	Format text
grep	Search a file for a pattern
head	Display the beginning (head) of a file
less	Show text, one screenful at a time
more	Show text, one screenful at a time
nl	Number lines
paste	Merge lines of text
pg	Show text, one screenful at a time
pr	Format and print text
sort	Sort and/or merge text
spell	Check for spelling errors
tail	Display last part of a file
tr	Translate characters
uniq	Display lines in a file that are unique
wc	Count number of lines, words, and characters in text

Table 10-2
Some UNIX filters.

10.11 Wildcards

Wildcards are also called metacharacters.

Typing and retyping file names can be a nuisance, especially if the names are long or there are very many of them. You can abbreviate file names using *wildcards*, which are characters that can stand for other characters (just as a joker in a pack of cards can stand for other cards in the pack).

The wildcard symbols are the asterisk (*), the question mark (?), and the square brackets [ ]. To see how these symbols are used, suppose that you had a directory named Fun containing the following files:

backgammon	backpacking	baseball	basketball
biking	blackjack	boxing	bridge
camping	canoeing	checkers	chess
crossword	dancing	eating	fencing
fishing	football	golf	hearts
hiking	karate	poker	rugby
sailing	skiing	softball	swimming
team1	team2	team3	team4
teamA	teamB	teamC	teamD
teamM	teamW	teamX	teamY
teamZ	track	wrestling	

The asterisk matches one or more characters.

The asterisk (*) is by far the most commonly used wildcard. It matches any character or string of characters, including blanks. As you can see, the directory Fun contains a large number of files. Using wildcards you can avoid having to list all of them when you are interested in just a few. For example, the command

§ ls f* (RETURN)

will list only those files beginning in *f*:

fencing fishing football

The command

§ ls *ball (RETURN)

will cause the shell to list the files that end in *ball*:

baseball basketball football softball

You are not limited to using a single asterisk. For instance, the command

§ ls *ack* (RETURN)

will list file names that contain the sequence of letters *ack:*

backgammon backpacking blackjack track

WARNING	THE ASTERISK WILDCARD MUST BE USED WITH CARE. THE rm * COMMAND, FOR EXAMPLE, CAN ERASE ALL OF THE FILES IN THE CURRENT DIRECTORY.

The question mark matches a single character.

The question mark (?) wildcard matches just one character at a time. For example,

§ ls ?iking (RETURN)
biking hiking

The brackets specify the character(s) to match.

The square brackets [ ] instruct the shell to match any characters that appear inside the brackets. For example

§ ls team[ABXYZ] (RETURN)
teamA teamB teamX teamY teamZ

You can also indicate a range of characters, rather than list each character:

§ ls team[1-4] (RETURN)
team1 team2 team3 team4

You can combine the wildcards *, ?, and [ ]. Suppose you wanted to list all of the files in the directory Fun that begin with the letters *a*, *b*, or *c*. This command will do the trick:

§ ls [abc]* (RETURN)

The bracketed letters tell the shell to look for any file names that have *a*, *b*, or *c* at the beginning. The asterisk matches any other sequence of letters. The result is the list

backgammon backpacking baseball basketball biking blackjack
boxing bridge camping canoeing checkers chess crossword

Likewise, to list all of the files having names that end with any letter from *m* through *z*, you could use the command

§ ls *[m-z] (RETURN)

The asterisk matches any sequence of characters; the brackets match only letters from *m* through *z* that appear at the end of the file name.

backgammon checkers chess hearts

10.12   Quoting Special Characters

You will recall that UNIX file names should not contain any of the following special characters:

& * \ | [ ] { } $ < > ( ) # ? ' " / ; ^ ! ~ %

By now it should be clear why: each of these characters has a special meaning to the shell. But sometimes this can be a problem. You may want to use a special character in its usual, everyday meaning. Consider, for example, the command line

§ echo What time is it? (RETURN)

The shell will interpret the question mark as a wildcard, and it will try to find a file name to match it. Unless you happen to have a file with a three-character name beginning with *it*, the shell will not be able to find a match, and it will complain:

§ echo: No match.

If you want the shell to treat a question mark as a question mark, not as a special character, you must quote it. One way to do this is to write a backslash (\) immediately before the question mark:

§ echo What time is it\? (RETURN)

> *Without the backslash, ? is treated as a wildcard.*

This produces the output

What time is it?

Note that the backslash does not appear in the output; its only purpose is to cancel the special meaning of the question mark.

The backslash only works on a single character. Thus, to produce the output

**** STARS ****

you would have to place a backslash in front of each of the special characters:

§ echo **** STARS **** (RETURN)

Quoting each special character individually can be tedious. Alternatively, you can quote the entire string of characters all at once using single quotes:

> *Without the single quotes, the asterisks would be treated as wildcards.*

§ echo '**** STARS ****' (RETURN)

The single quotes ('...') used here should not be confused with the backquotes (`...`). Backquotes, which are also called *grave* accent marks, are used to enclose commands that you want the shell to run. Thus, the command line

> *The backquotes run the date command.*

§ echo It is now `date`. (RETURN)

will produce output that looks something like this

It is now Mon Aug 13 16:04:41 EST 2007.

where the shell has run the date utility and included the result in the output from echo. In contrast, this is what would happen if you left off the backquotes:

§ echo It is now date. (RETURN)
It is now date.

> *Double quotes are less powerful than single quotes.*

Double quotes ("...") are like single quotes but less powerful. Putting double quotes around a string of characters cancels the special meaning of any of the characters except the dollar sign ($), backquotes (`...`), or backslash (\).

The different ways of quoting special characters are summarized in Table 10-3.

> **Table 10-3**
> Quoting special characters. Here, string represents any string of characters.

Quote	Effect
\	Cancel the special meaning of the next character
'string'	Cancel the special meaning of any characters in string
"string"	Cancel the special meaning of any characters except $, ``, and \
`string`	Run any commands in string; output replaces `string`

10.13 Background Processing

Processes that can run unattended are often put in the background.

As we said before, UNIX is a multitasking operating system, which means that it can run more than one program for you at the same time. You can start a command and put it in the "background," to continue running while you work on another task in the foreground.

Running a background process is simple: Type an ampersand (&) at the end of the command line before pressing (RETURN). Consider a hypothetical long-running program called longrun. You could run this program in background with the command

§ longrun & (RETURN)

If you were running the Bourne Shell, you would then see something like this:

3216 is the process identification number (PID).

3216
§

Running the C Shell, TC Shell, Korn Shell, or Bash, you would see something like this:

[1] is the job number; 3216 is the PID.

[1]   3216
§

Whichever shell you are using, it assigns a *process identification number* or PID to every process running in the background. The C Shell, TC Shell, Korn Shell, and Bash also assign a *job number,* which is the number in brackets. A prompt then lets you know that the shell is ready to process another command line, even if longrun is not yet finished:

§

The PID is important if you want to terminate a background job before it finishes. This is done with the kill command. To kill background process number 3216, for example, you would use the command

§ kill 3216 (RETURN)

Incidentally, some hard-to-kill processes require stronger medicine. Using kill with the -9 option will usually deal with them:

§ kill -9 3216 (RETURN)

Table 10-4
Job control commands. Here, *n* represents a job number.

Command	Effect
bg %*n*	Send process *n* to the background
fg %*n*	Bring process *n* to the foreground
jobs	List jobs
kill %*n*	Kill (terminate) process *n*
stop %*n*	Stop (suspend) process *n*

10.14 More Shell Features

The C Shell, TC Shell, Korn Shell, and Bash offer the same functionality as the original Bourne Shell. In addition, these shells include some features not present in the Bourne Shell:

■ **Job control.** All of the common shells allow you to run processes in the background with the ampersand (&) and eliminate them with the `kill` command. The C Shell, TC Shell, Korn Shell, and Bash also have *job control,* which makes it easier to manage background processes. Job control commands (Table 10-4) allow you to stop processes temporarily, move foreground processes to the background and back again, and kill processes.

■ **Command history.** The C Shell, TC Shell, Korn Shell, and Bash `history` mechanism maintains a list of the most recent commands you have entered, and gives you a convenient way to repeat a command from the list.

■ **Filename completion.** Using the *filename completion* feature (found in the C Shell, TC Shell, and Bash), you can type a command and part of a filename, then have the shell complete the filename for you.

These additional shell features are discussed in greater detail in Chapter 12.

10.15 Exercises

1. Be sure you can define each of the following terms:

shell	program	process
option	argument	standard input
standard output	grave accent	redirection
pipe	tee	filter
metacharacter	wildcard	quote
background process	foreground process	process id number
PID	job number	job control

2. What would each of the following commands do?

```
echo *
echo /*
echo \*
echo "*"
echo
echo */*
rm *        [Careful—do not try this!]
```

For Exercises 3–6, suppose your working directory contained the following files:

backgammon	backpacking	baseball	basketball
biking	blackjack	boxing	bridge
camping	canoeing	checkers	chess
crossword	dancing	eating	fencing
fishing	football	golf	hearts
hiking	karate	poker	rugby
sailing	skiing	softball	swimming
team1	team2	team3	team4
teamA	teamB	teamC	teamD
teamM	teamW	teamX	teamY
teamZ	track	wrestling	

3. How would you use cat to show the contents of the files ending in *ing*?

4. How would you list any files containing *x* or *X* (in this case, boxing and teamX)?

5. How would you show the contents of files with names containing *o*?

6. How would you show the contents of the files backgammon, backpacking, and blackjack using just one command?

Chapter

11

TUTORIAL: WORKING WITH THE SHELL

In this chapter, you will gain experience using the shell as a command interpreter. You will practice grouping commands; working with wildcards, filters, pipes, and tees; and running commands in the background.

11.1 Grouping Commands

First try grouping several commands on the same command line, using semicolons as command separators. Then redirect the output into a file:

1. Enter the commands on one line, separated by semicolons. You can print your working directory, the calendar for September 2007, and the current date and time with this command line:

§ pwd; cal 9 2007; date ⟨RETURN⟩

2. Run the same commands again, but redirect the output into a file. Be sure to put parentheses around the commands:

Without the parentheses, only the output from date would go into the file.

§ (pwd; cal 9 2007; date) > out1.tmp ⟨RETURN⟩
§

Nothing appears on the screen except the prompt because the output was redirected into out1.tmp instead of going to the standard output.

3. Use the cat command to check on the contents of the file.

§ cat out1.tmp ⟨RETURN⟩

You should see something like this:

```
/home/yourlogin
    September 2007
 S  M Tu  W Th  F  S
                   1
 2  3  4  5  6  7  8
 9 10 11 12 13 14 15
16 17 18 19 20 21 22
23 24 25 26 27 28 29
```

```
30
Sat Dec 29   13:21:46  MST   2007
```

11.2 Creating a File with cat

cat prints on the standard output the contents of any file(s) specified as arguments.

The cat command is one of the simplest—and most useful—of the UNIX utilities. You have already used cat to view and to combine ("catenate") files. As you will see in this section, cat can also serve as a "quick and dirty" alternative to a text editor.

1. Invoke cat without an input file, redirecting the output into the file you want to create. If cat is not given an input file to read, it reads from the standard input. Thus, to create a file named out2.tmp, type

```
§ cat  > out2.tmp (RETURN)
```

At this point, you should see nothing happening on the screen, because cat is waiting for you to enter text.

2. Type the text you want to put into the file. For example,

```
My Bonnie looked into the gas tank, (RETURN)
The contents she wanted to see. (RETURN)
I lit a match to assist her: (RETURN)
Oh, bring back my Bonnie to me! (RETURN)
```

3. Generate an end-of-file (EOF) signal. This is done by typing

```
(CONTROL) - (D)
§
```

The prompt tells you that cat has finished and you are back in the shell.

4. Check the file. The cat command will show that the text has been stored in the file:

```
§ cat out2.tmp  (RETURN)
```

You should see something like this:

```
My Bonnie looked into the gas tank,
The contents she wanted to see.
I lit a match to assist her:
Oh, bring back my Bonnie to me!
```

You can also indicate explicitly that you want cat to read the standard input by typing a hyphen (-) instead of a file name. Try it:

1. Invoke cat with a hyphen instead of an input file, redirecting the output into the file you want to create. Thus, to create a file named out3.tmp, type

The hyphen tells cat to read from the standard input.

```
§ cat - > out3.tmp (RETURN)
```

At this point, you should see nothing happening on the screen, because cat is waiting for you to enter text.

2. Type the text you want to put into the file. For example,

```
There once was a fellow named Frank, (RETURN)
who drove around town in a tank. (RETURN)
It was noisy and dark, (RETURN)
and quite hard to park, (RETURN)
But it got him good rates at the bank. (RETURN)
```

3. Generate an end-of-file (EOF) signal. This is done by typing

```
(CONTROL) - (D)
§
```

4. Check the file. The cat command will show that the text has been stored in the file:

```
§ cat out3.tmp  (RETURN)
```

You should see something like this:

Keep out1.tmp, out2.tmp, and out3.tmp—you will use them later in the chapter.

```
There once was a fellow named Frank,
who drove around town in a tank.
It was noisy and dark,
and quite hard to park,
But it got him good rates at the bank.
```

The cat utility is not a replacement for a text editor—cat does not allow you to change or delete text from a file—but it can be useful in creating short text files.

11.3 Using Wildcards

If you worked through the previous sections carefully, you should now have three new files in your directory named out1.tmp, out2.tmp, and out3.tmp.

■ **Examine the files using the cat command and the asterisk wildcard (*).** Thus, to view the files that begin in *out*, type

```
§ cat out*  (RETURN)
```

To view all of the files ending in *.tmp*, type the command line

```
§ cat *.tmp (RETURN)
```

■ **Examine the files using the cat command and the question mark (?).** Recall that the question mark matches any single character. Thus, to view the files out1.tmp, out2.tmp, and out3.tmp, type

```
§ cat out?.tmp  (RETURN)
```

The file names `out1.tmp`, `out2.tmp`, and `out3.tmp` differ only by one character—a number in the fourth position—and the question mark can stand for any of the numbers.

■ **Examine the files using the `cat` command and the brackets.** The brackets can be used to indicate a range of letters or numerals. To view the files `out1.tmp`, `out2.tmp`, and `out3.tmp`, type

§ `cat out[1-3].tmp` (RETURN)

11.4 Using wc

The `wc` ("word count") filter counts the lines, words, and characters in a file or collection of files. It has the following general form:

`wc [-lcw] filelist`

where `filelist` is a list of one or more file pathnames. You can apply various options so that `wc` prints only the number of lines (`-l`), or the number of words (`-w`), or the number of characters (`-c`). The `wc` command is very simple to use:

■ **Enter the `wc` command and the file name.** Try it on the `out2.tmp` file:

§ `wc *2.tmp` (RETURN)

This produces the output

```
4        27        133   out2.tmp
```

showing that there are 4 lines, 27 words, and 133 characters in the `out2.tmp` file. (To `wc`, a "word" is simply any group of characters followed by blanks, tabs, or newlines.)

■ **Run the `wc` command on multiple files.** Try this command line:

§ `wc *[2-3].tmp` (RETURN)

This runs `wc` on `out2.tmp` and `out3.tmp`, producing the output

```
4        27        133   out2.tmp
5        33        160   out3.tmp
9        60        293   total
```

Note that `wc` shows the line, word, and character counts for the files individually, as well as the totals for both files.

11.5 Using grep

The `grep` filter searches line by line through specified input files for a pattern of characters. Any line containing the desired pattern is printed on the standard output. The format of `grep` is

`grep [-cilnv]` *pattern* [*filelist*]

See Appendix D to learn about regular expressions.

The *pattern* may be a simple word or string of characters, or it may be a *regular expression*. A regular expression is a compact notation that specifies a general string of characters, in much the same way that a wildcard represents a set of file names. Regular expressions are discussed in Appendix D.

■ **Search for a particular word in a set of files.** Thus, to search the files `out1.tmp`, `out2.tmp`, and `out3.tmp` for lines containing the word *tank*, you would use the command

§ grep tank *tmp (RETURN)

Any lines containing the pattern *tank* are listed on the screen:

```
out2.tmp:My Bonnie looked into the gas tank,
out3.tmp:who drove around town in a tank.
```

■ **Search using the line-number option.** The -n option causes grep to print the number of any line containing the pattern:

§ grep -n tank *tmp (RETURN)

The word *tank* occurs on the first line of `out2.tmp` and on the second line of `out3.tmp`. Hence, grep prints

```
out2.tmp:1:My Bonnie looked into the gas tank,
out3.tmp:2:who drove around town in a tank.
```

■ **Search using the list-only option.** The -l option causes grep to list only the names of the files containing the pattern. For example,

§ grep -l Bonnie *tmp (RETURN)
out2.tmp

■ **Reverse the sense of the test.** The -v option causes grep to list the lines that do **not** contain the pattern. For example,

§ grep -v dark out3.tmp (RETURN)

```
There once was a fellow named Frank,
who drove around town in a tank.
and quite hard to park.
But it got him good rates at the bank.
```

11.6   Using sort

As you might expect, sort sorts the lines in a file or collection of files. It can also merge two or more files without sorting them. The sort command has the general format

Items in square brackets are optional.

sort [-bcdfimMnortuyz] [*-field*] [*filelist*]

As you can see, sort takes quite a large number of options, only a few of which will be discussed in this section. A *field* is a sequence of characters bounded by white space. (The individual words in a line of text might be considered as fields, for example.) Sorting is normally done according to the first field in each line, but you can specify that other fields be examined instead.

■ **Perform a simple sort on the first field of the files.** The following command line will list the sorted contents of out1.tmp, out2.tmp, and out3.tmp:

```
§ sort *.tmp (RETURN)
                             1
      September 2007
  2   3   4   5   6   7   8
  9  10  11  12  13  14  15
  S   M  Tu   W  Th   F   S
/home/yourlogin
 16  17  18  19  20  21  22
 23  24  25  26  27  28  29
 30
But it got him good rates at the bank.
I lit a match to assist her:
It was noisy and dark,
My Bonnie looked into the gas tank,
Oh, bring back my Bonnie to me!
Sat Dec 29   13:21:46 MST   2007
The contents she wanted to see.
There once was a fellow named Frank,
and quite hard to park,
who drove around town in a tank.
```

The sorting order is also called the *collating sequence*.

This may appear strange until you understand the sorting order that the sort utility employs. This varies from system to system, but the following is typical:

1. Control characters

2. White space (i.e., blanks and tabs)

3. Numerals

4. Uppercase letters

5. Lowercase letters

You can apply various options to modify the sorting order. Here are just a few possibilities:

sort -b	Ignore leading blanks
sort -f	Fold upper- and lowercase letters together (ignore case)
sort -n	Numeric sort (e.g., 1 precedes 10)
sort -r	Reverse usual order (e.g., Z precedes a)

■ **Sort on the first field, ignoring leading blanks and case.** Specifying a field off-set of +0 will cause sort to examine the first field of each line:

```
§ sort -bf +0 *.tmp ⟨RETURN⟩

/home/yourlogin
                 1
16 17 18 19 20 21 22
 2  3  4  5  6  7  8
23 24 25 26 27 28 29
30
 9 10 11 12 13 14 15
and quite hard to park.
But it got him good rates at the bank.
I lit a match to assist her:
It was noisy and dark,
My Bonnie looked into the gas tank,
  Oh, bring back my Bonnie to me!
 S  M Tu  W Th  F  S
Sat Dec 29   13:21:46  MST   2007
    September 2007
The contents she wanted to see.
There once was a fellow named Frank,
who drove around town in a tank.
```

■ **Sort on the second field of the files.** Specifying a field offset of +1 will cause sort to skip the first field of each line and examine the second field. Try this on the file out3.tmp:

```
§ sort -bf +1 out3.tmp ⟨RETURN⟩

who drove around town in a tank.
But it got him good rates at the bank.
There once was a fellow named Frank,
and quite hard to park.
It was noisy and dark,
```

There is much more to the sort utility than we can detail here. If you want to know more, refer to the UNIX manual.

11.7 Pipes and Tees

A pipe connects the standard output from one utility to the standard input of another utility. A tee allows you to take the output from a command and direct it into a file and to another command. In this section, you will practice using pipes and tees.

■ **View the calendars for 2007 and 2008, one page at a time.** One of the following command lines will do:

```
§ (cal 2007; cal 2008) | more ⟨RETURN⟩
```

Or

§ (cal 2007; cal 2008) | pg (RETURN)

■ **View the calendars for 2007 and 2008, and create a file containing these calendars.** This requires a tee and two pipes:

§ (cal 2007; cal 2008) | tee calfile | more (RETURN)

■ **List the files in the root's subdirectories, one page at a time.** Either of the following commands will work to pipe the output from ls to the more or pg utility:

§ ls -a /* | more (RETURN)

or

§ ls -a /* | pg (RETURN)

■ **List the files in the root's subdirectories and create a file containing this listing.** This can be done using two pipes and a tee:

§ ls -a /* | tee root.list | more (RETURN)

This places a list of the root and its subdirectories into the file root.list as this list is also displayed on the terminal screen.

■ **Count the files in the root's subdirectories.** This can be done with the command line

§ ls -a /* | wc -l (RETURN)

■ **Print a long listing of the root's subdirectories, sorted by size (largest first).** The fifth field in a long listing gives the file size. To perform a reverse numerical sort (-rn) on the fifth field, skip the first four fields (+4):

§ ls -al /* | sort -rn +4 | more (RETURN)

■ **Make a long listing of the root's subdirectories; sort it by size; send it to the standard output and to a file.** The fifth field in a long file listing normally shows the size of the file. To sort on the fifth field, skip the first four fields (+4):

§ ls -al /* | sort -n +4 | tee list.by.size | more (RETURN)

■ **Find a file among the root's subdirectories.** Thus, to find the file passwd, enter the command line

§ ls -a /* | grep passwd (RETURN)

11.8 Sleeping

The sleep command creates a process that "sleeps" for a specified period of time. In other words, sleep waits a specified number of seconds before returning to the shell. It has the general format

```
sleep n
```

Exercise 1 deals with the
accuracy of the sleep
command.

where n is a nonnegative integer that indicates the number of seconds the process
is to sleep. On most systems, the sleep utility does not count seconds very
accurately, so n is only an approximation.

1. Run the sleep command. To sleep for about 15 seconds, enter

§ sleep 15 (RETURN)

2. Use sleep to delay execution of another command. This is a common appli-
cation of the sleep utility. For example,

§ (sleep 60; echo I am awake now) (RETURN)

3. Wait for the process to finish. When sleep finishes, echo will print

I am awake now

11.9   Interrupting a Foreground Process

If you start a long-running process such as sleep the usual way (that is, in the
foreground), you cannot work on any other commands until it finishes. If for
some reason you do not wish to wait that long, you must interrupt the process.
This is done with the (CONTROL) - (C) key combination.

1. Start the process. For example,

§ (sleep 120; echo I am awake now) (RETURN)

2. Interrupt the process. Type

(CONTROL) - (C)

This will interrupt sleep and invoke the echo command:

```
^CI am awake now
§
```

11.10   Running a Background Process

As we said before, UNIX allows you to run a process in the "background" while
you work on another task in the foreground. This is useful for long-running
processes, especially those that do not require your attention. As an example of
such a long-running process, we will once again use the sleep command.

1. Start a long-running process in the background. For example,

§ (sleep 60; echo I am awake now)& (RETURN)

If you are running the Bourne shell, you should see something like this:

The number you see will
likely be different.
3271

In this example, the shell assigned a process identification (PID) number of 3271. (The actual PID on your system may be different.)

If you are running C Shell, TC Shell, Korn Shell, or Bash, you should see

The numbers you see will
likely be different.

```
[1]      3271
```

Here, [1] is the job number and 3271 is the PID.

The shell will display a prompt to let you know it is ready for more commands:

```
§
```

2. Check status of the process. Enter the ps ("process status") command to check on what is happening:

```
§ ps (RETURN)
```

You might see something like this (the PIDs will be different):

```
PID   TTY   TIME    COMMAND
3140  p0    0:01    sh
3271  p0    0:00    sleep 60
3290  p0    0:00    ps
§
```

Note that there are three processes: the shell (sh in this example); sleep; and the ps command itself.

3. Wait for the process to finish. After approximately 60 seconds, you should get the message:

```
I am awake now
§
```

11.11 Killing a Background Process

Sometimes it is necessary to terminate a background process. This is done with the kill command. To see how this works, try the same background process you used in the previous section.

1. Start the background process. Be sure to note the PID:

```
§ (sleep 60; echo Stop this command) &  (RETURN)
3310
§
```

2. Kill the process. Type kill, a space, and the PID number:

```
§ kill 3310 (RETURN)
```

Some systems will tell you when a background job has been killed:

```
Terminated  (sleep 60; echo Stop this command)
§
```

11.12 Command Summary

Counting Lines, Words, and Characters

wc *file(s)*	count lines, words, and characters in *file(s)*
wc -1 f*ile(s)*	count the lines in *file(s)*

Searching

grep *pattern file(s)*	print line(s) in *file(s)* containing *pattern*
grep -n *pattern file(s)*	as before, but print line numbers as well
grep -1 *pattern file(s)*	print the name of any file containing *pattern*
grep -v *pattern file(s)*	print line(s) *not* containing *pattern*

Sorting

sort *file(s)*	sort *file(s)* observing the usual collating sequence
sort -b *file(s)*	sort, ignoring leading blanks
sort -f *file(s)*	sort, folding lowercase and uppercase together (ignore case)
sort -n *file(s)*	sort numerically (1 before 10, etc.)
sort -r *file(s)*	reverse sort (9 before 0, Z before A, *etc.*)
sort +*n file(s)*	sort on field $n + 1$ (skip n fields)

Sleeping

sleep *n*	sleep *n* seconds

Foreground and Background Processing

^C	interrupt (kill) a foreground process
^D	generate end-of-file signal
^Z	stop (suspend) a foreground process
command &	run command in background
ps	obtain process status
kill *n*	terminate background process *n*

11.13 Exercises

1. How accurately does the sleep command count seconds? Try the following command to find out:

```
(date; sleep 60; date)
```

2. Refer to the man entry for cat to determine what each of the following commands is supposed to do:

```
cat -e file
cat -s file
cat -t file
cat -u file
cat -v file
cat -vet file
```

3. Refer to the man entry for grep to determine what each of the following commands is supposed to do:

```
grep -c pattern file
grep -i pattern file
grep -l pattern file
grep -n pattern file
grep -v pattern file
```

4. Refer to the man entry for sort to determine what each of the following commands is supposed to do:

```
sort -d
sort -m
sort -M
sort -n
sort -o
sort -r
sort -t
sort -u
sort -y
sort -z
sort -nr
```

5. The -R ("recursive") option causes ls to list not only the files in the specified directory, but also the files inside any subdirectories. How could you use this with an appropriate pipe-and-filter arrangement to determine whether a file exists in your account?

TUTORIAL:
LOGGING IN REMOTELY

Running either `rlogin` or `telnet` on your local UNIX host, you can work on a remote computer system on which you have an account. The difference is that `rlogin` allows you to connect only to another UNIX system; `telnet` can connect to UNIX and non-UNIX hosts.

`rlogin` and `telnet` are security risks. Secure alternatives are discussed in Part VI.

Both `rlogin` and `telnet` transmit data (including passwords) in readable form. To prevent someone from intercepting and reading your data, some system administrators replace `rlogin` and `telnet` with a secure alternative such as Secure Shell (SSH).

22.1 Running rlogin

In this section you will see how to use `rlogin` to log into your account on a remote UNIX host. (If you do not have an account on another machine, you can practice with your local account.)

1. Start the `rlogin` program, specifying the remote host and your remote login name. Thus, if you had an account named `jsmith` on the remote UNIX host `merlin.podunku.edu`, you would type

§ `rlogin merlin.podunku.edu -l jsmith` `(Return)`

On some systems, that will be enough to get you into the remote system; no password is needed. Other systems will require that you enter a password:

`password:`

2. If necessary, enter the password that you use for the remote host. This may not be the same as the password used on your local host.

3. When you finish working on your remote account, log out from that account. One of the following commands should work (see Chapter 3):

§ `logout` `(Return)`

§ `exit` `(Return)`

§ `(CONTROL)`-`(D)`

22.2 Running telnet

In this section you will see how to use `telnet` to log into a remote host—either a UNIX or non-UNIX computer—on which you have an account. (If you do not have an account on another machine, you can practice with your local account.)

1. Start the `telnet` program.

§ `telnet` (Return)

You will receive the `telnet` prompt:

`telnet>`

2. Enter the Open command, followed by the Internet address of the remote machine. Thus, if you had an account on `merlin.podunku.edu`, you would type

`telnet> open merlin.podunku.edu` (Return)

The `telnet` program will try to connect to the remote host. If the connection is successfully made, the remote host will display a login prompt:

```
Trying . . .
Connected to merlin.podunku.edu.
Escape character is '^]'

SunOS UNIX (merlin.podunku.edu)
login:
```

3. Log into your remote account. Follow the procedure set out in Chapter 3, "Getting Started." Once you have logged in, you can run the usual UNIX commands (but not the X Window System) on the remote host.

22.3 telnet Commands

When you logged in using `telnet`, you probably noticed a message about an "escape character" that may have looked something like this:

`Escape character is '^]'`

This means that the `telnet` program uses the (Control)-(]) key combination as an escape sequence. (This is not to be confused with the (Esc) key that is used with the `vi` editor.) The `telnet` escape character allows you to suspend your work on the remote host and give commands to the `telnet` program itself.

1. Enter the `telnet` escape character. On most systems, this is the ^] combination:

§ (Control)-(])

The computer will respond with the `telnet` prompt:

`telnet>`

2. Display the list of `telnet` **commands.** Enter a question mark (?) at the prompt:

`telnet> ?` (Return)

The program will respond with a list of commands:

```
close     close current connection
display   display operating parameters
mode      line-by-line or character-at-a-time mode
open      connect to a site
quit      exit telnet
send      transmit special characters
set       set operating parameters
toggle    toggle operating parameters
z         suspend telnet
?         print help information
```

3. Display a detailed command description. To get more information on any of these commands, type the command name followed by a question mark:

`telnet> close ?` (Return)

The `telnet` program will show you a description of the `close` command:

`close  closes current connection`

That does not tell you anything more than you already knew. However, some of the other commands give you considerably more information; take a moment and try them out.

4. Exit the `telnet` **command mode.** This is done by pressing the (Return) key at the telnet prompt:

`telnet>` (Return)

This will put you back into your remote UNIX account.

22.4   Ending the telnet Session

Once you have finished working on the remote host, you should log out from that machine and end the `telnet` session.

1. Log out from your remote account. This is done the usual way (see Chapter 3). One of the following commands should work:

§ `logout` (Return)

§ `exit` (Return)

§ (CONTROL)-(D)

When you have logged out, you will see a `telnet` prompt:

```
telnet>
```

At this point you could, if you wish, open another remote session using the open command.

2. Quit the `telnet` program. Enter `quit` at the prompt:

```
telnet> quit (Return)
```

You will see a UNIX shell prompt:

§

22.5 A Shortcut Method

There is a quicker way to run a `telnet` session:

1. Enter the `telnet` command, followed by the Internet address of the remote machine. Thus, if you had an account on the host computer `merlin.podunku.edu`, you would type

```
§ telnet merlin.podunku.edu (Return)
```

Eventually, you will see the `login` prompt:

```
login:
```

2. Log into your remote account as usual.

3. When finished, close the connection.

```
telnet> close (Return)
```

This will usually log you out of the remote account and quit `telnet`. You should see a UNIX shell prompt:

§

22.6 Connecting to Guest Accounts

Normally, you must have an account on any remote host to which you want to connect using `telnet`. However, a number of special `telnet` accounts exist on the Internet to provide services to the public. There are two ways to log into such an account.

The first—and perhaps most common—method requires that you connect to the host computer using `telnet`, then log into the account using a special login name and password. (Many systems do not require a password.) For example, you can reach the online catalog of the Washington State University library this way:

```
§ telnet griffin.wsu.edu (Return)
```

When you reach the server, it will prompt you for a login:

```
login:
```

The login to be used is library; no password is required for this particular service.

The second method is to use telnet to log into the server through a special "port," designated by number. It is usually unnecessary to provide either a login or password. For example, Melvyl, the University of California's on-line catalog can be reached using the command line

§ telnet melvyl.ucop.edu 23 (Return)

Note the number 23; this is the port number.

22.7 Command Summary

Each of these commands is typed in after the UNIX prompt, and each is terminated by a (Return). The address of the remote host is represented by *host*.

Remote Login Commands (UNIX shell prompt)

rlogin *host*	log into a remote UNIX computer named *host*
telnet *host*	log into a remote computer named *host*
telnet	start up the telnet program

Telnet Commands (Telnet Prompt)

open *host*	open connection to computer *host*
?	print telnet help
close	close connection to remote host
quit	quit telnet session

22.8 Exercises

1. If you have an account on a remote UNIX machine, log into that account using rlogin.

2. If you have an account on a non-UNIX machine that is connected to the network, log into that account using telnet.

3. Use telnet to connect to the Washington State University library.

4. Use telnet to connect to Melvyl at the University of California.

TUTORIAL: TRANSFERRING FILES

Both rcp ("remote copy") and ftp ("file transfer protocol") allow you to transfer files between two computer systems on which you have accounts. The rcp utility is designed to work with two UNIX systems; ftp can also get files from non-UNIX hosts. Moreover, ftp can be used to obtain files from public file servers.

Many system administrators replace rcp and telnet utilities with secure alternatives.

Secure alternatives to rcp and telnet are discussed in Part VI.

23.1 Running rcp

In this section you will see how to use rcp to obtain a file from a remote UNIX host. For rcp to work, three conditions must be met:

■ You must have an account on the remote UNIX host.

■ Both hosts must "trust" each other. (That is, certain files exist on each host listing the other as being trustworthy.)

■ You must have permission to copy the file.

Assuming that these conditions are met, the procedure for copying the file is very simple:

■ **Enter the** rcp **command, specifying the remote host and remote file, then the local host and the new file name.** For example, if you wanted to copy the file *myfile* from the remote UNIX host *farhost*, you would type

§ rcp *farhost*:*myfile mycopy* (Return)

The name of the remote host is separated by a semicolon from the pathname of the file on the remote host. Note that no password is needed. The rcp utility will simply refuse to work if you do not have an account on the remote host or the hosts do not trust each other.

23.2 Running ftp

In this section you will see how to use `ftp` to copy files from a remote host—either a UNIX or non-UNIX computer—on which you have an account.

1. Start the `ftp` program.

§ ftp (Return)

You will receive the `ftp` prompt:

ftp>

2. Enter the `open` command, followed by the Internet address of the remote machine. Thus, if you had an account on `farhost.xyz.edu`, type

ftp> open farhost.xyz.edu (Return)

The `ftp` program will try to connect to the remote host. If the connection is successfully made, the remote host will prompt for your login name:

```
Connected to farhost.xyz.edu.
220 farhost.xyz.edu FTP server (Version 4.179) ready.
Name (farhost.xyz.edu):
```

3. Enter your login name. Be sure to use the login name for the remote account, not that on your local account, if they are different. For example, if you had an account named `smithj` on the remote host, you would type

Do not enter `smithj` (unless that is your login). Enter *your* login here.

```
Name (farhost.xyz.edu): smithj (Return)
```

The remote host will prompt for your password:

```
331 Password required for smithj
Password:
```

4. Enter your password. Of course, the password does not show on screen as you type it.

Enter your password here; it will not appear on the screen. ——————

```
Password:
```

You will be notified when you have successfully logged in:

```
230 User smithj logged in.
ftp>
```

23.3 ftp Help

The ftp program takes dozens of commands. Fortunately, one of those commands is help, which lists and describes the set of ftp commands.

1. Enter the help command at the ftp prompt. There are two ways to do this. Either type the word help, or a single question mark (?):

ftp> ? (Return)

The computer will respond with a list of commands:

!	dir	nput	rmdir
$	disconnect	nmap	runique
account	form	ntrans	send
append	get	open	status
ascii	glob	prompt	struct
bell	hash	proxy	sunique
binary	help	sendport	tenex
bye	lcd	put	trace
case	ls	pwd	type
cd	macdef	quit	user
cdup	mdelete	quote	verbose
close	mdir	recv	?
cr	mkdir	remotehelp	
delete	mls	rename	
debug	mode	reset	

Some of these are similar to UNIX commands that are already familiar to you (such as cd, ls, mkdir, and pwd). Others are peculiar to the ftp program.

2. Obtain a description of a command. Enter the help or ? command, followed by the command you are interested in. For example, to get a description of the delete command, enter the command line

ftp> ? delete (Return)

The program will respond with a short description of the command that will give you an idea of how it is used:

delete   delete remote file

23.4 Getting a File

One of the reasons to use ftp is to get a copy of a file from a remote host. This is done with the get command.

1. Move to the remote directory containing the file you want. Like the UNIX shell, `ftp` uses the `cd` command to change the working directory. Thus, if you wanted to get a file from the subdirectory `Marsupials`, you would type

Enter the pathname of the directory containing the file you want.

```
ftp> cd Marsupials  (Return)
```

Depending on how `ftp` has been set up on your system, you may see a message that looks something like this:

```
250 CWD command successful.
```

2. List the files to find the one you want. With `ftp`, as with the UNIX shell, you can do this with the `ls` command:

```
ftp> ls  (Return)
```

This command will list the files in the current directory on the remote host. It usually tells you how many bytes of information were transferred across the network:

```
200 PORT command successful.
150 Opening ASCII mode data connection for file list.
bandicoot
kangaroo
opossum
wombat
226 Transfer complete
38 bytes received in 0.0042 seconds (8.9 Kbytes/sec)
```

3. Select the file transfer mode. As far as `ftp` is concerned, there are two types of files. An *ASCII file* contains text; a *binary file* contains other kinds of information (such as graphics, audio recordings, or compressed text). Depending on the type of information that is in the file, enter either `ascii` or `binary` at the `ftp` prompt:

```
ftp> ascii  (Return)
```

The `ftp` program will confirm your selection:

```
200 Type set to A.
>
```

4. Get the file. Enter the `get` command, followed by the name of the original file, then the name you want to give the local copy. For example, suppose you want to get a copy of the file `wombat` from the remote host, and that you want to name it `wombat.copy` on your local host. You would enter this line:

```
ftp> get wombat wombat.copy  (Return)
```

In most cases, `ftp` will inform you that the transfer was successful:

```
200 PORT command successful.
150 Opening ASCII mode data connection for wombat (7014
```

```
bytes)
226 Transfer complete
7224 bytes received in 0.8 seconds (8.8 Kbytes/sec)
ftp>
```

23.5   Sending a File

Using ftp, you can also send a file from your local host to the remote host—the reverse of the operation described in the previous section. This is done with the put command.

1. Specify the file type. Remember, ftp distinguishes between ASCII files containing text and binary files containing other kinds of information (graphical, audio, etc.). Select the proper file transfer mode by entering either ascii or binary at the ftp prompt:

```
ftp> ascii (Return)
```

The ftp program will confirm your selection:

```
200 Type set to A.
>
```

2. Send the file. Enter the put command, followed by the name of the original file, then the name you want to give the remote copy. For example, suppose you wanted to send a copy of the file meeting.events from the local host, and that you want to name it meeting.events.copy on your remote host. You would enter this line:

```
ftp> put meeting.events meeting.events.copy (Return)
```

ftp will inform you that the transfer was successful:

```
200 PORT command successful.
150 Opening ASCII mode data connection for meeting.events
226 Transfer complete
local: meeting.events   remote: meeting.events.copy
2878 bytes received in 0.033 seconds (86 Kbytes/sec)
ftp>
```

23.6   Ending the ftp Session

Once you have finished working on the remote host, you should end the ftp session.

■ **Quit the ftp program.** Enter quit at the ftp prompt:

```
ftp> quit (Return)
```

You will see a UNIX shell prompt:

§

23.7 A Shortcut Method

There is a quicker way to run an `ftp` session:

1. Enter the `ftp` command, followed by the Internet address of the remote machine. Thus, if you had an account on the host `farhost.xyz.edu`, you would type

§ ftp farhost.xyz.edu ⏎(Return)

2. Log into your remote account as usual. This will require that you enter your login and password at the appropriate prompts.

3. When finished, close the connection using the `quit` command.

ftp> quit (Return)

This will log you out and quit `ftp`. You should see a UNIX shell prompt:

§

23.8 Getting Files with Anonymous ftp

Originally, `ftp` was intended to allow you to transfer files between two computers on which you have accounts. However, *anonymous* `ftp` allows you to get files from hosts on which you do not have an account. These hosts are called *public ftp servers*.

For example, the United States Census Bureau maintains a server that you can reach by anonymous `ftp`.

1. Start the `ftp` program and specify the server you want. For example, to connect to the Census Bureau's public `ftp` server, you would enter the command

§ ftp ftp.census.gov (Return)

When you reach the server, it will identify itself and prompt for your login name:

```
Connected to ftp.census.gov.
220-          U.S. Department of Commerce, Bureau of Census
220-*****************************************************
```

Various warning and disclaimers appear here. ─────────────────────────

```
220 blue.census.gov FTP server ready.
Name (ftp.census.gov:yourlogin):
```

2. Enter the guest login name at the prompt. Some servers expect you to enter "`guest`" as your login; others require "`anonymous`." For the Census Bureau server, use "`anonymous`":

The server will notify you that it has accepted the login name; it may also prompt you for a password:

Some servers require you to enter "guest" as your login name.

`Name (ftp.census.gov:yourlogin): anonymous` (Return)

```
331 Guest login ok, send e-mail address as password.
Password:
```

3. If necessary, enter the guest password. Some systems require no password; others use "guest" or "anonymous." The Census Bureau server asks for your e-mail address. Thus, if your address were `jsmith@merlin.podunku.edu`, you would enter this at the prompt:

Enter the required guest password here; it will not appear on the screen.

`Password:`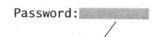

4. Use `ftp` commands to find and transfer files.

5. When you are finished, quit `ftp` as before.

23.9 File-Compression Programs

Large files are often compressed to save storage space and decrease the time needed to transfer them over the network. Depending on the file and the compression technique, a compressed text file may occupy as little as 40% of the memory required by the original.

A compressed file is typically distinguished from a normal file by a file name suffix, which indicates the program that was used to compress the file. Some of the more common compression/decompression programs, and their file name suffixes, are listed in Table 23-1.

Table 23-1
File compression/de-compression programs.

Compression	Decompression	Suffix	Sample File Name
compress	uncompress, zcat	.Z	textfile.Z
cpio	cpio	.cpio	textfile.cpio
gzip	gunzip	.gz	textfile.gz
pack	unpack	.z	textfile.z
pax	pax	.pax	testfile.pax
Stuffit	unsit	.Sit	textfile.Sit
Packit	unpit	.pit	textfile.pit
PKZIP	PKUNZIP	.ZIP	textfile.ZIP
tar	tar	.tar	textfile.tar

Strictly speaking, cpio, tar, and pax are not compression programs; they are *file archive programs*. Such programs can combine a number of files and directories into a single file—called an *archive file*—for storage on tape or transferring across the Internet. An archive file is often compressed before it is transferred.

Of the programs listed above, compress and tar are the ones most commonly found on UNIX systems. The procedure for preparing a file or set of files for compression using tar and compress is fairly straightforward, as you will see in the next few sections.

23.10 Creating an Archive File

The tar program is normally used to prepare multiple files and directories for storage or transfer. If you are working with just one file, you will probably not bother with tar; in that case, skip this section.

1. Create an archive file using tar. To archive all of the files in a directory, run the tar program with the -cf option, giving a name for the archive file and specifying the directory that is to be processed. Thus, to create an archive file named marsupials.tar containing the files from the Marsupials directory, you would enter

Here, -c means "create"; f
peceeds the tar file.   § tar -cf marsupials.tar Marsupials (Return)

2. Check that the tar **file has been created.** Enter the ls command to list the files:

§ ls (Return)

You should see the names of both the original directory and the tar file:

Note that tar does not alter
the original directory.   Marsupials marsupials.tar

3. Verify the contents of the tar **file.** This is done with the -t ("table of contents") option:

§ tar -tf marsupials.tar (Return)

The tar program will list the files that were bundled together to make the archive file. Next, the tar file will need to be compressed.

23.11 Compressing Files

The most common compression program found on UNIX systems is compress, which is very simple to operate:

1. Compress the file. This is done by typing the compress command, followed by the name of the file to be compressed:

§ compress marsupials.tar (Return)

2. Check that the compressed file has been created. Once again, enter the ls command to list the files:

§ ls (Return)

You should see the names of both the original directory and the newly compressed file:

Marsupials marsupials.tar.Z

The compress program attaches the .Z suffix automatically.

Once you have compressed the file, it is ready to be transferred by ftp. When using ftp to send a compressed file, be sure to specify binary (not ascii) file transfer type.

23.12 Uncompressing Files

Once the compressed file has been transferred to its destination, it must be uncompressed. The uncompress command is used to restore files that have been processed with compress. If you are working with a compressed tar file, you should uncompress it before untarring it.

1. Enter the uncompress command, followed by the name of the file to be restored. The file should have the .Z suffix:

§ uncompress marsupials.tar.Z (Return)

2. List the files. The compressed file will be gone, replaced by its uncompressed version:

§ ls (Return)
marsupials.tar

In this example, the uncompressed file is an archive (tar) file; you must "untar" it to convert it back into a directory.

23.13 Restoring tar Files

The tar command is used with the -x ("extract") option to restore an archive file:

1. If necessary, create a directory to hold the untarred files. In this case, create a directory named Marsupials2:

§ mkdir Marsupials2 (Return)

Some versions of tar do not allow the -C option, but put the untarred file in the current directory.

2. Enter the Extract command. Type tar -xf, followed by the name of the tar file, the -C ("change directory") option, and finally the name of the directory where you want the untarred directory to go:

§ tar -xf marsupials.tar -C Marsupials2 (Return)

3. Check the directory. The newly untarred Marsupials directory should appear inside the Marsupials2 directory:

§ ls Marsupials2 (Return)
Marsupials

If you list the contents of the Marsupials directory, you should see the files contained.

23.14 Command Summary

Each of the UNIX commands listed here is typed at the shell prompt and terminated by (Return). Each of the ftp commands is typed at the ftp prompt and terminated by (Return).

Remote Copy Command (UNIX shell prompt)

rcp *farhost*:*file* *mycopy*   copy *file* from *farhost* as *mycopy*

File Transfer Commands (UNIX shell prompt)

ftp *farhost*   log into a remote computer named *farhost*

ftp   start up the ftp program

ftp Commands (ftp Prompt)

open *farhost*   open connection to computer *farhost*

?   print ftp help

get *file* *mycopy*   get remote *file*; save locally as *mycopy*

put *file* *mycopy*   send local *file* to remote host as *mycopy*

quit   close connection to remote host

tar Commands (UNIX Shell Prompt)

tar -cf *file.tar* *Dir*   make tar file *file.tar* from directory *Dir*

tar -tf *file.tar*   print table of contents for *file.tar*.

tar -xf *file.tar* *Dir*   extract file(s) from *file.tar* to directory *Dir*

compress Commands (UNIX Shell Prompt)

compress *file*   compress *file* (creates file named *file.Z*).

uncompress *file.Z*   restore *file.Z*

23.15 Exercises

1. Be sure you can define the following terms:

anonymous `ftp`	archive file	ASCII file
binary file	`tar` file	

2. Use `ftp`'s `help` command to determine what the following commands do:

`append`	`mdelete`
`bell`	`mdir`
`bye`	`mkdir`
`cd`	`mls`
`cdup`	`nput`
`delete`	`pwd`
`dir`	`recv`
`disconnect`	`remotehelp`
`lcd`	`rmdir`
`ls`	

3. Information on NASA and its programs can be obtained by anonymous `ftp` from the host `explorer.arc.nasa.gov`. Log in as "anonymous" and try to get a list of Frequently Asked Questions (FAQ) related to the requirements for becoming an astronaut.

4. Genealogical information can be obtained by anonymous `ftp` from the host `ftp.cac.psu.edu`. Log in as "anonymous" and see if you can obtain a list of useful tips for beginning genealogists.

5. Larry Landweber, a computer scientist at the University of Wisconsin, collects data on international network connectivity. He maintains a list of the countries that are connected to the Internet, BITNET, FIDONET, or `uucp`. Obtain this list by anonymous `ftp` from `ftp.cs.wisc.edu`. (Hint: Look for a directory named `connectivity_table`.)

TAMING YOUR TERMINAL

The stty ("set terminal") command allows you to set parameters that affect the operation of your terminal. In this appendix you will see how to use stty to perform the following tasks:

- Set your terminal to handle lowercase input.

- Define the erase key.

- Ensure that the terminal echoes your input properly.

A.1 Correcting Uppercase-Only Output

Sometimes the system may behave as if your terminal can handle only uppercase letters. (This can occur if you accidentally press the "Caps Lock" key before logging in.) The following command will correct the problem:

§ STTY -LCASE (RETURN)

A.2 Defining the Erase Key

Most users expect the (BACKSPACE) key to erase characters on the command line. (Others prefer to use (DELETE) or (CONTROL)-(H) for this.) The following command will make (BACKSPACE) the character-erase key:

§ stty erase (BACKSPACE) (RETURN)

The following command will set (DELETE) as the character-erase key:

§ stty erase (DELETE) (RETURN)

To set the (CONTROL)-(H) key combination as the character-erase key, use the command line

§ stty erase ^h (RETURN)

Note that the caret (^) is used to represent the (CONTROL) key.

A.3 Setting the Terminal Echo

As you type characters on the keyboard, the system is supposed to echo them back to you on the terminal screen (except when you are entering your password). If what you type does not appear on the screen, you can turn on the echo using the following command:

§ stty echo (RETURN)

On the other hand, if every character is being echoed **twice**, you should turn off the echo:

§ stty -echo (RETURN)

Appendix

B

THE UNIX MANUAL

The UNIX system is described in detail in a massive document called the UNIX Programmer's Manual or User's Reference Manual, or simply the User's Manual. Your UNIX installation may have a printed (paper) copy of this manual, an on-line (electronic) version, or both.

The UNIX manual has the reputation of being difficult to read. It has been said that if you can read the manual, you do not need the manual. That is a bit of an exaggeration, but the manual is terse and takes some getting used to. Even so, it is a good idea to get familiar with the manual — it can be very useful.

B.1 Organization of the Manual

Most UNIX manuals have eight sections:

Section 1   User Commands

Section 2   UNIX and C System Calls

Section 3   Library Calls

Section 4   Device Drivers and Special Files

Section 5   File Formats and Conventions

Section 6   Games

Section 7   Miscellany

Section 8   System Administration Commands and Procedures

Your system's manuals may be arranged a bit differently. (For example, it is not uncommon to find that some spoilsport has deleted the games from the system.)

In addition to the usual eight manual sections, you may find supplementary articles and technical papers describing the UNIX system. These are usually grouped together and called something like "Documents for Use with the UNIX System," or "UNIX User's Supplement," or perhaps "UNIX Programmer's

Manual, Volume 2." We won't say much about this second part of the manual—if you happen to find a copy, you might want to browse through it to see if it contains anything of interest to you.

B.2 Using the man Command

If your system has an on-line manual, you can read it using the man command, which has the general form

§ man *command* (RETURN)

For example, to read the manual entry for the cal command, you would type

§ man cal (RETURN)

If your system has an on-line manual, this command will list a man page for cal, as shown in Listing B–1.

```
CAL(1)                    USER COMMANDS                    CAL(1)

NAME
      cal - display a calendar

SYNOPSIS
      cal [ [ month ] year ]

DESCRIPTION
      cal displays a calendar for the specified year. If
      a month is also specified, a calendar for that
      month only is displayed. If neither is specified,
      a calendar for the present month is displayed.

      year can be between 1 and 9999. Be aware that 'cal
      78' refers to the early Christian era, not the
      20th century. Also, the year is always considered
      to start in January, even though this is
      historically naive.

      month is a number between 1 and 12.

      The calendar produced is that for England and her
      colonies.


      Try September 1752.
```

Listing B-1
The manual page for the cal command.

B.3 Organization of a Manual Entry

All manual entries follow much the same format. Let's examine the various parts of the entry for the `cal` command:

- CAL(1)   USER COMMANDS   CAL(1)

The first line begins and ends with the name of the command, written entirely in caps (CAL). The number in parentheses (1) gives the section of the manual in which this entry is found.

- NAME
      cal - display a calendar

The name and a one-line description of the command are listed next.

- SYNOPSIS
      cal [[**month**] **year**]

This is probably the most useful part of the man page. It shows how the command is actually used. Anything shown in square brackets [] is optional. In this case, the brackets show that you can use the `cal` command either by itself, with the year only, or with the month and year. Thus, each of the following commands would be legal:

§ cal (RETURN)
§ cal 2001 (RETURN)
§ cal 5 2001 (RETURN)

Some commands take various options, which are typically preceded by a hyphen. The options will be shown here, along with the other arguments.

- DESCRIPTION

Next comes a written description of the command. This description may be as short as a paragraph, or it may go on for several pages, depending on the command.

B.4 Other Categories

The manual entry for the `cal` command is rather simple because the `cal` command itself is rather simple. Entries for other commands may contain still more headings. Depending on the command, you may see one or more of the following:

- FILES—Files used or created by the command are listed here under this heading.

- SEE ALSO—This entry will direct you to other entries in the manual that are related to the current topic.

■ DIAGNOSTICS—Some UNIX commands generate error messages. The more important or cryptic error messages will be described under this heading.

■ BUGS—Believe it or not, some UNIX commands contain minor errors—usually called "bugs"—that have been identified but yet not eliminated. If you are lucky, such bugs will be listed here.

B.5 Reading Longer Manual Pages

The manual entry for `cal` will probably fit entirely on your screen. Other manual entries are too long to be shown on the typical terminal screen all at once. For example, try reading the manual entry describing `man` itself:

§ man man (RETURN)

If the entire manual entry is too long to fit on the screen, you can pipe the output from the `man` command through the `more` or `pg` utility:

§ man man | more (RETURN)

or

§ man man | pg (RETURN)

The vertical line is called the *pipe symbol*.